Volume IX
Publication No. 97
November 1976

Mysticism: Spiritual Quest or Psychic Disorder?

Formulated by the
Committee on Psychiatry and Religion

Group for the Advancement of Psychiatry

This publication was produced for the Group for the Advancement of Psychiatry by the Mental Health Materials Center, Inc., New York.

Additional copies of this GAP Publication No. 97 are available at the following prices: 1–9 copies, $4.00 each; 10–24 copies, list less 15 per cent; 25–99 copies, list less 20 per cent; 100–499 copies, list less 30 per cent.

Upon request the Publications Office of the Group for the Advancement of Psychiatry will provide a complete listing of GAP titles currently in print, quantity prices, and information on subscriptions assuring the receipt of new publications as they are released.

Orders amounting to less than $5.00 must be accompanied by remittance. All prices are subject to change without notice.

Please send your order and remittance to: Publications Office, Group for the Advancement of Psychiatry, 419 Park Avenue South, New York, New York 10016.

Standard Book Number 87318-134-4

Library of Congress Catalog Card Number 76-45931

Printed in the United States of America

TABLE OF CONTENTS

This is the seventh in a series of publications comprising Volume IX. For a list of the other GAP publications on current topics of interest, see last page of book herein.

STATEMENT OF PURPOSE

THE GROUP FOR THE ADVANCEMENT OF PSYCHIATRY has a membership of approximately 300 psychiatrists, most of whom are organized in the form of a number of working committees. These committees direct their efforts toward the study of various aspects of psychiatry and the application of this knowledge to the fields of mental health and human relations.

Collaboration with specialists in other disciplines has been and is one of GAP's working principles. Since the formation of GAP in 1946 its members have worked closely with such other specialists as anthropologists, biologists, economists, statisticians, educators, lawyers, nurses, psychologists, sociologists, social workers, and experts in mass communication, philosophy, and semantics. GAP envisages a continuing program of work according to the following aims:

1. To collect and appraise significant data in the fields of psychiatry, mental health, and human relations
2. To reevaluate old concepts and to develop and test new ones
3. To apply the knowledge thus obtained for the promotion of mental health and good human relations

GAP is an independent group, and its reports represent the composite findings and opinions of its members only, guided by its many consultants.

MYSTICISM: SPIRITUAL QUEST OR PSYCHIC DISORDER? *was formulated by the Committee on Psychiatry and Religion, which acknowledges on page 711 the participation of various individuals in the preparation of this report. The members of this committee, as well as the other committees and officers of GAP, are listed below.*

COMMITTEE ON PSYCHIATRY AND RELIGION

Sidney S. Furst, Bronx, N.Y., Chr.
Stanley A. Leavy, New Haven
Richard C. Lewis, New Haven

Albert J. Lubin, Woodside, Calif.
Mortimer Ostow, Bronx, N.Y.
Michael R. Zales, Greenwich, Conn.

COMMITTEE ON ADOLESCENCE

Warren J. Gadpaille, Englewood, Colo., Chr.
Maurice R. Friend, New York
Charles A. Malone, Philadelphia
Silvio J. Onesti, Jr., Belmont, Mass.

COMMITTEE ON AGING

Prescott W. Thompson, San Jose, Chr.
Gene David Cohen, Rockville, Md.
Charles M. Gaitz, Houston
Lawrence F. Greenleigh, Los Angeles
Maurice E. Linden, Philadelphia
Robert D. Patterson, Lexington, Mass.
F. Conyers Thompson, Jr., Atlanta
Jack Weinberg, Chicago

COMMITTEE ON CHILD PSYCHIATRY

Virginia N. Wilking, New York, Chr.
Paul L. Adams, Miami
E. James Anthony, St. Louis
James M. Bell, Canaan, N.Y.
Harlow Donald Dunton, New York
Joseph Fischoff, Detroit
Joseph M. Green, Tucson, Ariz.
John F. Kenward, Chicago
Ake Mattsson, Charlottesville
John F. McDermott, Jr., Honolulu
Theodore Shapiro, New York
Exie E. Welsch, New York

COMMITTEE ON THE COLLEGE STUDENT

Malkah Tolpin Notman, Brookline, Chr.
Robert L. Arnstein, Hamden, Conn.
Harrison P. Eddy, New York
Varda Peller Ganz, Palo Alto
Gloria C. Onque, Pittsburgh
Elizabeth A. Reid, Cambridge, Mass.
Kent E. Robinson, Towson, Md.
Earle Silber, Chevy Chase, Md.
Tom G. Stauffer, White Plains, N.Y.

COMMITTEE ON THE FAMILY

Joseph Satten, San Francisco, Chr.
C. Christian Beels, Bronx, N.Y.
Ivan Boszormenyi-Nagy, Wyncote, Pa.
Murray Bowen, Chevy Chase
Henry U. Grunebaum, Boston
Margaret M. Lawrence, Pomona, N.Y.
David Mendell, Houston

Carol Nadelson, Boston
Norman L. Paul, Boston

COMMITTEE ON GOVERNMENTAL AGENCIES

Sidney S. Goldensohn, Jamaica, N.Y., Chr.
William S. Allerton, Richmond
Albert M. Biele, Philadelphia
Harvey L. P. Resnik, Chevy Chase, Md.
Harold Rosen, Baltimore
Harvey Lee Ruben, New Haven
William W. Van Stone, Palo Alto

COMMITTEE ON INTERNATIONAL RELATIONS

Bryant M. Wedge, Washington, D.C., Chr.
Francis F. Barnes, Chevy Chase
Eric A. Baum, Cambridge
Alexander Gralnick, Port Chester, N.Y.
Rita R. Rogers, Torrance, Calif.
Bertram H. Schaffner, New York
Mottram P. Torre, New Orleans
Roy M. Whitman, Cincinnati
Ronald M. Wintrob, Hartford

COMMITTEE ON MEDICAL EDUCATION

Paul Tyler Wilson, Bethesda, Md., Chr.
Raymond Feldman, Boulder, Colo.
Saul I. Harrison, Ann Arbor
Harold I. Lief, Philadelphia
John E. Mack, Chestnut Hill, Mass.
Herbert Pardes, Brooklyn, N.Y.
Robert Alan Senescu, New York
Jeanne Spurlock, Silver Spring, Md.
Bryce Templeton, Philadelphia
Sidney L. Werkman, Denver
Sherwyn M. Woods, Los Angeles

COMMITTEE ON MENTAL HEALTH SERVICES

W. Walter Menninger, Topeka, Chr.
Allan Beigel, Tucson, Ariz.
Eugene M. Caffey, Jr., Washington, D.C.
Merrill T. Eaton, Omaha
Joseph T. English, New York
James B. Funkhouser, Richmond, Va.
Robert S. Garber, Belle Mead, N.J.
Alicia Gavalya, Allston, Mass.
Donald J. Scherl, Boston
Herzl R. Spiro, Princeton, N.J.
Jack A. Wolford, Pittsburgh

708

COMMITTEE ACKNOWLEDGMENTS

The Committee would like to express its appreciation to two consultants, Professors Joseph Campbell, of Sarah Lawrence College, and Gerson D. Cohen, Chancellor of Jewish Theological Seminary, for providing much expert information and orientation during the initial phase of this study.

In particular we wish to recall and to acknowledge the very many contributions which John Higgins made to this and to previous studies. Dr. Higgins was a founding member of our Committee and was serving as its chairman at the time of his death.

We are indebted to past committee members Drs. Earl Loomis, Jr. and Bernard Pacella, and to committee guests, Drs. Angelo D'Agostino and Arthur Deikman, who participated for varying periods during the preparation of this report. We are also grateful to three Ginsburg Fellows who worked with us: Drs. Sister Vincent Ferrer Charles and Richard Jaeckle participated actively during their two-year fellowships, and Dr. Clyde Snyder contributed to the final phase of our work.

PREFACE

The interest of the Committee on Psychiatry and Religion in producing a report on mysticism derives from the fact that mysticism has become a significant social force in our time. The primary purpose of the report is to contribute to an understanding of *the psychology of mysticism.* This objective was pursued by the Committee's examination of recurrent patterns and features in the long history and complex phenomenology of mysticism.

Of necessity, considerable selectivity must mark any attempt to pinpoint causes and effects in the broad panorama unfolded by the known history of mysticism in the world's religions. It was therefore considered beyond the scope of our inquiry to sift through all the world's religions for some evidence of significant mystical component. Accordingly, this report has concentrated on a brief historical survey of mystical trends and movements as they have occurred in the Jewish, Christian and Hindu religions, with a description of three individual mystical movements that were selected for illustrative purposes and to provide a perspective of the field. A more comprehensive survey would have to consider Islamic and most Eastern religions, as well as the religions of preliterate cultures in much of Africa, Central and South America, East Asia, and the Arctic Circle. These have been excluded in favor of examples from the Jewish, Christian and Hindu religions because the Christian and Jewish religions are more familiar to a readership largely drawn from the Judeo-Christian culture, and because Hinduism is more closely related to current Western mystical movements.

Any attempt to understand mysticism must take into account the fact that the disposition of both individuals and groups to turn to mysticism is influenced by environmental factors. Social, cultural, economic, political and religious conditions all play a significant part, not simply in attracting

713

the individual to mysticism, but in determining the origin and the fate of mystical movements. These environmental conditions vary from one sociocultural group to another, and also from one time period to another for the same group. While assessment of these factors takes the psychiatrist away from his area of special expertise, he cannot disregard them. This report, therefore, is addressed to those who would like to consider a psychiatric view of the psychology of mysticism.

INTRODUCTION

Evidence for the existence of mysticism and mystical trends is to be found in the history of most societies, both "primitive" and civilized. This fact alone compels the conclusion that mysticism serves certain psychic needs, or that it constitutes an attempt to resolve certain ubiquitous problems. One or another of these purposes will in turn be reflected in the characteristics of the mystical movement, the mystical experience, and the mystic himself.

One can say of the mystic that he is an individual who views the world differently from others. To varying degree, the mystic derogates and detaches himself from the perceived real world. He does so in either or both of two ways: First, he attributes a greater reality to his inner world, or to a belief in a transcendental or supernatural world. This suggests a similarity with schizophrenic detachment. It differs in that for the mystic the detachment from consensual reality is deliberately sought, while for the schizophrenic it appears to be obligatory. Second, he attributes a higher reality or value to certain aspects of the perceived world, along with a complementary derogation of others. This resembles both the hallucinogenic drug experience and the temporal lobe seizure.*

In attempting to account for these phenomena, the psychiatrist may assume that what is derogated or denied is disturbing, while what is elevated and valued is desired. Though he may employ drugs to facilitate or intensify the mystical experience, the mystic usually achieves his goal by psychological means alone; the hallucinogenic drug user by

---

* *temporal lobe seizure:* a seizure state initiated by a discharge in the temporal lobe of the brain and characterized by automatic action, by disturbance of consciousness, by disordered perception including illusion and hallucination, or by any combination of these. During the seizure the individual seems detached from the usual continuum of his conscious mental state.

pharmacologic means; while the temporal lobe seizure is attributable to organic factors.

From the psychiatric point of view, the mystical experience and the mystical way of life will be examined for information regarding psychic organization and function, both normal and pathologic. We shall consider a number of hypotheses derived from biographical and historical data concerning individual mystics and mystical movements. Let us begin by defining or at least describing mysticism.

1

WHAT MYSTICISM IS

The word *mystical* is used to describe experiences that have for their goal a union with a supernatural power, in contrast to other experiences which are more appropriately called "magical," "esoteric," "visionary," "occult" or "metaphysical." Differing from the usual practices of institutional religions, mysticism involves a relationship with the supernatural which is not mediated by another person; the goal of mystical union is reached during the course of this relationship. The union itself is considered ultimate reality, compared with which the events of everyday life are dim and uncertain.

The mystic asserts that the experience of union is not achieved by rational intellectual functions or through the ordinary senses, but from the depths of the soul. He is driven toward his goal by an outgoing love for the supernatural object. Although his description may employ sexual metaphors to describe this love, he asserts that it is not the sexually contaminated love of a man for a woman. Neither is it the self-seeking love of a child.

There is probably a mystical element in all institutional religions—at least for some adherents. The tendency of the mystical approach to isolate individuals, or to alienate them from established authority, is one of the reasons that churches tend to discourage it, inasmuch as they are dependent on social organization. On the other hand, a mystical leader may dominate a religious group. In cases of "secular" mysticism, it may be denied that the practice is religious in nature, although here we become involved with questions of definition.

Mystical experiences vary widely in content, but they share certain characteristics. The basic technique for achieving the mystical goal, used by mystics of all times and places, is commonly called contemplation. Successful contemplation requires arduous practice. Through it the mind gradually finds ways of eliminating thoughts of the self and the ordinary world as well as abandoning all imaginative or reasoning thought processes. The ultimate direct encounter with the supernatural—the unitive state—occurs during a period of mental emptiness. It appears, as it were, on a blank screen. Although the mystic has worked hard to find his way there, he feels that he is a passive recipient of the event.

The training process often begins with meditation—an exercise in which thought is consciously restricted to an isolated aspect of the potential mystic's belief system: a single sacred word, one aspect of God, or a short passage from the Bible, for example. All other ideas are rejected. This type of thinking is gradually succeeded by a state of emptiness in which rational thinking processes are eliminated, comparable to the alteration of consciousness that follows sensory deprivation in experimental studies. During this "quiet" period, the mystic becomes aware of the supernatural while remaining distinct from it; an awareness of the self as an independent agency continues to exist. The state of true contemplation, or union, follows.

There are two aspects of the contemplative state, the transcendental and the immanent; they differ in relative strength from one mystic to another. Perceived from the transcendental aspect, the supernatural object is "the wholly other" or "the Cloud of Unknowing"—the numinous; feelings of strangeness and awe in relation to it predominate, with corresponding feelings of humility concerning the self. On the other hand, a belief in the immanent nature of the supernatural, conceived as a part of the self, contributes to a more intimate and more joyful relationship with it.

The ultimate in the contemplative state, although not essential to it, is the occurrence of an ecstatic trance. The mystic is physically transfixed, unable to move or speak, and he experiences a tremendous lucidity. A state of rapture is differentiated from the state of ecstasy on the basis of its sudden, violent onset and the occurrence of gross mental disorganization.

Great mystics, like great artists, take advantage of the ideas of their historical forebears, even though their search is private and creative. They usually have been adherents of traditional religious groups and make use of the religious forms to which they have been exposed. While doing so, however, their private and creative nature often puts them on a course that defies traditional practices, and they may find themselves at war with established authority.

Mystics agree that the mystical experience is ineffable, yet often they have felt the need to explain it. In reading the literature of the mystics, it is well to bear in mind that when attempting to describe the indescribable they have been forced to use symbolic terms. Images likening the mystic to the pilgrim, the lover, or the alchemist are among those which have been commonly used. Mystical writers stress the inadequacy of such symbolic language and warn the reader of its dangers and limitations. They excuse their recourse to it on the ground that no other language is available to them.

The natural history of the contemplative process tends to follow a more or less typical course that has been called "the Mystic Way."[1] It is marked by alternating periods of joy and suffering. Indeed, suffering is considered essential to the attainment of the unitive state. Typically, the Mystic Way is inaugurated by the sudden onset of an exalted experience known as conversion. Mystical conversion, which should be distinguished from the usual conversion to a religious belief, is characterized by the sudden expansion of the mystic's frame of reference from a narrow, self-centered state to a broader view of himself in the world and a beginning awareness of the transcendent. This stage, as well as others of the Mystic Way, may be accompanied by visions or voices, a radiant light, and an increased lucidity involving one or all of the senses.

Clearly aware of his imperfections in relation to the supernatural, the mystic may now enter the state of purgation, a state that is filled with pain and suffering. In it he attempts to purify himself by ascetic self-mortification: He simplifies his existence, leads a life of poverty and chastity, and detaches himself from worldly pursuits and desires.

Once the mystic has succeeded in this initial divestment of his impurities and sensual claims, he emerges—both symbolically and literally—from the darkness into a bright light; this is the state of illumination. Suffering is again replaced with joy. There is a heightening of the sense perceptions and an apprehension of the supernatural. This is not as complete as in the later stage of union, since the self is still perceived as a distinct entity. Auditory and visual hallucinations, and phenomena such as automatic writing, commonly appear during this phase.

A typical example among Western mystics is that described by Saint Teresa of Avila:

> Though I have visions of angels frequently, yet I see them only by an intellectual vision. It was our Lord's will that in this vision I should see the angel in this wise. He was not large, but small in stature, and most beautiful—his face burning, as if he were one of the highest angels, who seem to be all on fire. . . . I saw in his hand a long spear of gold, and at the iron's point there seemed to be a little fire. He appeared to me to be thrusting it at times into my heart, and to pierce my very entrails; when he drew it out, he seemed to draw them out also and to leave me all on fire with a great love of God.

> The pain was so great that it made me moan; and yet so surpassing
> was the sweetness of this excessive pain that I could not wish to be rid
> of it. The soul is satisfied now with nothing less than God.[2]

Typically, illumination is followed by the most painful and horrifying experience of the Mystic Way. The bright light, the lucidity, and the perception of the supernatural object are replaced by a great darkness, a feeling of having been abandoned by the object, and a conscious rejection of personal satisfactions. Similar to the earlier stage of purgation, it is deeper and more terrifying. The mystic, deprived and abandoned, feels so empty that contemplative activity is no longer possible and the visions and voices of the illuminative phase usually disappear. The emotions that accompany this period have caused it to be called the "mystic death" or "the dark night of the soul." It carries on the purification of the stage of purgation to its ultimate end, the total abandonment of any desire for self-satisfaction.

Thus prepared, the chosen few finally reach the mystical goal of union, a state of joy and absolute certainty. The actual experience is said to be timeless, yet often lasts for only a moment—"the space of an Ave Maria," according to St. Augustine. It remains forever implanted in the mystic's being. It is spontaneous, but at the same time the product of a long and difficult process. Although the mystic says that he seeks no reward for his labors, he feels that his outgoing love has been returned in kind and that he achieves an "ineffable peace" and a sense of moral perfection.

The mystic who conceives of the supernatural object as an awesome, distant figure is apt to describe this union in terms of a godlike transformation (called deification). When the supernatural is seen as a personal, intimate companion, the mystic may speak of a "spiritual marriage between God and the soul." Once having attained this peak experience, brief as it may be, the mystic is enabled to live his life henceforward on transcendental levels of reality. Endowed with great vitality and great certitude about the nature of his experience, the former recluse may now emerge as an active leader who regards the salvation of the world as his duty—not surprising, in view of his identification with a godlike figure. It should be emphasized that all mystics do not reach this state of union. Jewish mystics, for example, describe only a clinging to God, rather than a merging with Him.

The mysticism of the East insists on still another step along the mystical path: total annihilation of the self and its absorption into the Infinite, as expressed in the Sufis' Eighth Stage of Progress and the Buddhists' Nirvana. This suggests that the ultimate goals of Western and Eastern mysticism have opposing values: The Western mystic seeks the active life as a god-like figure or as one assisted by God, while the Eastern mystic seeks total passivity. It should be noted, however, that some Eastern mystics, Buddhists in particular, direct their mysticism into useful work and proselytizing.

The mystical groups currently active in the United States show varying degrees of identification with the older groups and traditions of both the East and the West. Some adhere closely to the readings and practices of a parent movement; others have adopted doctrines and disciplines with modifications; still others, while acknowledging past influence, emphasize innovation and creativity.

References

1. Evelyn Underhill. MYSTICISM (New York: E. P. Dutton, 1961).
2. Quoted in *ibid.*, 12th ed., pp 292-293. [Original from THE LIFE OF ST. TERESA OF JESUS, written by herself.]

2

THE CURRENT MYSTICAL SCENE

In confronting the current mystical scene in this country, one is struck by an almost bewildering profusion of leaders and their movements which are, or claim to be, ways leading to some degree of unitive mystical experience. A classification of these is perhaps most easily made according to whether their origins are oriental or occidental. That is, they are rooted within one or another of the Eastern religious traditions or within some aspect of Judeo-Christian culture. Any overview of this collage of mystical practice must of necessity be somewhat arbitrary in its inclusions. Nevertheless, some brief descriptions are in order.

Sects of Eastern Inspiration

To begin with the oriental groups, it is probable that the first major body in this country was the VEDANTA SOCIETY, established here in 1893 by the late Swami Vivekenanda, a disciple of the Indian mystic Shri Ramakrishna. Though within the Society there is some devotion to Ramakrishna himself, its main teaching effort is to expound the doctrines coming originally from the Vedas, the earliest Indian Scriptures. Basically it is a nondualistic philosophy which designates the Brahman as the ultimate reality of all existence. Since every person partakes of Brahman in his essential nature, by mystical practice one can attain to this realization. By comparison with some of the other groups described here, it is rather

723

sober and restrained. A number of prominent intellectuals have been attracted to it, among them Aldous Huxley and Christopher Isherwood.

A much less rigorous and exacting group are the followers of the MEHER BABA, an Indian guru claiming to be the avatar of incarnation for the current era. The center of the movement in this country is in Myrtle Beach, South Carolina. Its chief dogma is the acceptance of Meher Baba as God. Interestingly, from 1927 until his death in 1969, Baba remained silent and communicated only with hand gestures. As opposed to the previous group, there is here great emphasis on a founding personality. Mystical practice in this group has as its aim uniting with the figure of Meher Baba, and followers speak of his personality as then entering their lives.

The most famous Eastern movement in recent years has been that founded by MAHARISHI MAHESH YOGI, who became extremely popular here in the mid-1960s. He was one of the first of the guru leaders to denounce drugs as a way to awareness. Numerous popular idols like the Beatles singing quartet and actress Mia Farrow espoused his teachings with great publicity, and for a time he was one of the more photographed people around. Hundreds of training centers sprang up, many of them on college campuses.

Basically, the movement teaches a kind of meditation technique based on mantric concentration; this involves the repeating over and over to oneself of a preselected word or syllable and then noting whatever comes to consciousness. Some experimental work has indeed shown that in the course of this practice there is "a quieting of the mind," as suggested by a marked increase in the amount and amplitude of alpha rhythm recorded on the electroencephalogram, although skeptics claim that the alpha rhythm is no stronger at such times that it is when the subject is sitting quietly without focusing his attention on anything. Not infrequently, followers claim to experience a feeling of loss of self and attainment of cosmic unity by this practice. One of the chief distinctions of the movement has been the reducing of mantric meditation to an easily teachable technique, and this may partially account for its appeal to Westerners; it can be taught in a few sessions.

A much smaller but nonetheless visible group is the KRISHNA CONSCIOUSNESS movement, whose adherents, mostly young and clad in saffron robes, can be seen dancing and begging in the streets of large cities. Much of their public behavior seems naïve and childlike, and though some ecstatic experience is induced by the dancing and by group interaction, it appears to be deemphasized in favor of communal living and evangelizing.

A recent Indian guru achieved a considerable American following at the age of fifteen as THE CHILD GOD, Sri Guru Mahara-Ji, whose Divine Light Mission is headquartered in Hardwar, India. He succeeded his father, who died in 1966; the movement now claims 4,000,000 followers who see him as the chosen revealer of God in this age, similar to Christ or Buddha. Again, there is immense emphasis on the person of the leader. Followers frequently enter trance states in the contemplation of his picture as well as in his actual presence. Recently, Mahara-Ji's mother, living in India, has challenged his fitness to lead the movement.

Another group that is possibly more rigorous than the Vedantists is that founded by the Tibetan Lama Tarthang Tulka, who came to California in 1969 following the invasion of his country by China. A small number of his disciples are centered principally at the Tibetan Nyingmapa Meditation Center in Berkeley, California. At this center instruction is given in TANTRIC BUDDHISM, that branch of Buddhism traditionally practiced in Tibet and Mongolia. Physical rigors are emphasized and stress is laid on the transformation of the whole person on the way to Enlightenment. The aim, essentially a mystical one, is the negation of personal separateness and the attainment of unity transcending "I" and "other." A separate Tibetan Buddhist group, with centers in Vermont and Colorado, has aims similar to those of the Tulka group but accepts the leadership of Chogyam Trungpa Rinpoche, also a refugee lama.

Following the introduction of Vedanta, various Indian Yoga teachers with headquarters in India have opened centers around the world. These persons generally teach Hatha or physical Yoga as a beginning, leading more advanced students into meditative aspects of Raja Yoga, that variety of Yoga which stresses spiritual development via intellectual activity. Two examples of such groups are those established by Sri Arubindo and Swami Vishnudevananda.

Dating from the years immediately following the Second World War and coming from Japan is the ZEN BUDDHIST movement, begun largely in the United States by Daisetz Suzuki. In the past decade, meditation centers have been established in San Francisco and in Rochester, New York. A retreat house at Tassajara, California, is flourishing. There is some variation in practice between the two main schools, the Rinzai and the Soto, but regular and long meditation is the core of this discipline, which has as its aim the achievement of satori, or enlightenment—a unitive mystical experience. Here, as with some of the other movements, the end of the process is a mystical experience. Zen has persisted as one of the better-known movements in recent years, although, like Vedanta and Tibetan Yoga, the very arduousness of its practice has tended to limit the number of active long-term disciples.

In the past several years a number of SUFI GROUPS have made their appearance, all representing the mystical side of the Islamic faith. Idris Shah, a Sufi living in England, is probably the best known and most prolific writer on Sufism. The largest group in this country is headed by Pir Vilayat

Inayat Khan, and a particular feature of its practice is the attainment of ecstatic states through group movement and dance.

Also from the Near East comes the movement begun by G. I. GURDJIEFF, an itinerant Russian sage who wandered through Central Asia in search of Sufi and other masters and who came to Paris and New York after the Russian Revolution with a rather eclectic enlightenment system. The aim here is to awaken the disciple from his usual waking state of "sleep" to a higher level of consciousness, primarily through a recollective technique called "self-remembering." Mental operations here are too intellectual to allow for much mystical experience, but trance states have been reported.

The list of movements with Eastern origins briefly described here could be expanded considerably but it should give some idea of those currently active.

Sects of Western Origin

Turning to the West, the number of groups currently active is smaller. However, each of the major Western religious traditions—Catholic, Protestant and Jewish—has given rise to active mystical bodies.

Among Catholics, the various groups known collectively as CATHOLIC PENTECOSTALS have become active over the last decade. Typically, these meet for what is called an Agape, in which considerable importance is placed on the generation of strong emotional ties. *Agape*, as used here, means a communal meal or love feast at which there is felt to be mutual love and sharing of inner experience among members. Glossolalia* and ecstatic experiences are certainly accepted and sometimes sought. The love feasts are seen as a return to a more primitive, emotional and vital Christianity. It is be-

* *glossolalia,* literally "speaking in tongues," refers to the utterance of a religious message in spontaneous neologistic language.

lieved that some of the members develop a special insight into the needs and aspirations of the other members and thus acquire a counseling or teaching role within the group, but this bears no relation to their position in the Church hierarchy, since they generally come from the laity.

Within Protestantism, most of the old fundamentalist and evangelical ecstatic groups are still active. In the last few years there has sprung up a very loosely organized movement referred to collectively as the Jesus Movement, or THE JESUS PEOPLE. They bear strong resemblance to the earlier evangelical groups in their emphasis on the acceptance of Christ as personal savior and are made up mostly of adolescents and young adults. Here, too, ecstatic experiences are common, particularly in the setting of group worship. One body called the Children of God is rather more strict than other Jesus People in that members are enjoined to relinquish their names and all earthly possessions to the group. They have this in common with the Krishna Consciousness movement. In general, the Jesus People forbid or at least disapprove of drugs, alcohol, and extramarital sexual intercourse, but as with the Catholic Pentecostals, high value is placed on strong affective discharge and sharing as reflecting a return to a more vital and meaningful Christianity.

Within Judaism, the various HASSIDIC GROUPS, all of which spring from the Orthodox Jewish tradition, are the carriers of the main mystical current. These groups all have their roots in Eastern Europe and most of them are dynastic in that their current leader is generally selected by his predecessor. Emphasis in Hassidism is on an immediate and vital relation to God expressed in prayer and the fulfillment of religious obligations. Recently, notably within the Lubavitcher group, there has been a particular emphasis on mystical elements in an attempt to win back Jewish youth who have become adherents of non-Jewish mystical bodies.

One movement that may at first glance seem to be out of

place in a catalogue of mystical groups is the **biofeedback movement.** One of the objectives of biofeedback is to modify the output of cortical rhythm* and autonomic functioning† so as to induce states akin to those seen in classical meditation. These are states of predominantly alpha and theta rhythms, alpha being the physiologic rhythm associated with relaxation and theta that associated with creative fantasy and hypnagogic imagery.‡ Yogis and Zen masters in meditation have been found to produce strong alpha rhythms.

Last but not least are the various movements within **the drug culture** which make use of consciousness-altering drugs to achieve mystical experience. The oldest such body in the United States is the Native American Church, an American Indian group which, from its beginning, used peyote in its ecstatic rituals. Then there is the rather loosely organized movement initially popularized by Timothy Leary in the mid-1960s which used hallucinogens like LSD as a way toward mystical and/or religious experience. A number of religious groups have attempted to heighten states of religious experience by experimenting with the use of drugs in their particular religious context. It should be noted that almost without exception the religious groups outside the drug culture have condemned the use of drugs in achieving mystical states. In this respect, religious mystics using drugs are very much in opposition to those who do not.

The foregoing provides a sampling of what is available to the seeker after mystical experience. Rather than multiply examples further, it is perhaps more important to try to gain some understanding of why mysticism seems to be flourishing at this time in history.

---

* *cortical rhythm* refers to the electric pattern produced by the brain cortex.
† *autonomic functioning* refers to physiologic effects which are mediated by the autonomic nervous system.
‡ *hypnagogic imagery* refers to images which are perceived immediately before sleep.

Certainly the mystical experience has been valued
throughout history and in diverse cultures. It is also true that
certain times and places seem to have been more congenial to
the widespread search for mystical experiences. For example, during the first to the nineteenth centuries of the Christian era there were several periods when Christian mysticism
was cultivated. To quote Underhill, "This curve exhibits
three great waves of mystical activity besides many minor
fluctuations. They correspond with the close of the Classical,
the Medieval and the Renaissance periods in history, reaching their highest points in the third, fourteenth and seventeenth centuries."[1] Thus Underhill sees periods of more
generalized mystical activity as coming after and completing
an era of intellectual, political and literary flowering. For her,
mysticism serves as the high and crowning point to a period
of great human achievement.

One may look at the data in a different way, however, and
see a turning toward mysticism as a turning away from previously held belief and ordering systems about the nature of
reality and man. According to this view, contemporary
people, or at least many young people, are in a state of
disillusionment with the scientific and economic Weltan-
schauung and have reacted by moving inwardly to a more
spiritual and renunciatory way of life.

The one view sees the mystic and his way as the final
flowering of an historical period during which the achieve-
ments of the outer world are taken inward and in a sense
metamorphosed to a state of spiritual consciousness. The
other view perceives the mystic as turning aside in a renunciation of or disillusionment with the inadequate solutions
and chaos surrounding him to an inner fantasy life. Thus
there is both an introversion and a valuing of intrapsychic
life paralleled by a concomitant withdrawal of interest in the
life around him. Taken together, these two processes result
in a period of introversion in which, by a kind of alchemy,

the individual seeks to transform himself. Externally, as may be seen in our own time, when such an intensification occurs, it is during the breaking up of an old order.

Perhaps it is inevitable that the mystic is at odds with his environment, that opposition is necessary if any inward movement is to occur. At the same time, it is likely that without some valuing of the external world, the inner renunciation is likely to result in a sterile or depressive kind of inner experience. Accordingly, it is probable that those mystics who maintain good object relations show less psychopathology than those who do not maintain them.

Among those mystics who show unmistakable psychopathology, few will consult a psychiatrist as long as the mystical defense remains effective. However, at some point and often recurrently, the mystical defense breaks down. Then troublesome neurotic symptoms may appear, or possibly frank depression or psychosis. The psychiatrist who has been called upon to deal with such a situation must decide whether to attempt symptomatic relief—for example, with drug therapy or reassurance—or to undertake a searching psychoanalytic treatment which may threaten the individual's mystical commitment and life style. The psychiatrist will find mystical phenomena of interest because they can demonstrate forms of behavior intermediate between normality and frank psychosis; a form of ego regression in the service of defense against internal or external stress; and the paradox of the return of repressed aggression in unconventional expressions of love.

Although the adherents of mystical movements express sentiments to which most of society pays respect, their behavior, nevertheless, can be distressing to large segments of the population. Devoting oneself to new or foreign sects often expresses a repudiation and rejection of the religion of the family in which the young person grew up. The striving for improvement in the world is usually associated with an attack on society or on existing social institutions and current ways of life. Especially striking are those instances in which young people, having engaged for a period in promiscuous behavior, experience a conversion and join a mystical religious sect, embracing abstinence with the same fervor which formerly marked their pursuit of sensual pleasure. Rather than being pleased at this turn of events, the parents are usually dismayed. As sinners, the young people were violating community standards, but as saints they injure their parents by repudiating them and their religion, preferring the religion of strangers. The anger of the young person comes out in both of these techniques for dealing with frustration and threatening depression—that is, in sensual indulgence at one time, and religious devotion at another.

Any attempt to account for the current increased interest in mysticism should be based on some acquaintance with the long history of mysticism. The mystical groups and movements which have most influenced today's adherents will therefore be reviewed briefly.

Reference

1. Evelyn Underhill. MYSTICISM (New York: E. P. Dutton, 1961) p 454.

3

JEWISH MYSTICISM

As a discipline of study and instruction, Jewish mysticism represents an effort to penetrate the secret of the hidden and unseen God. In its earliest forms, as we find it in the written records of approximately the third century of this era, Jewish mysticism consists of a visual experience reserved for the elect, who, as a result of their consummate piety and esoteric learning, are able to ascend to the heavenly divine throne, or to some area of the heaven very near it. The ecstatic experience is one of seeing the hidden mysteries of the heavens, the angels ministering to God, and the Godhead Itself. In that respect, the earliest records of Jewish mysticism reflect an exegetical* expansion of the ecstatic prophetic visions of the sixth chapter of Isaiah and of the visions described in the first, third and tenth chapters of Ezekiel. The earliest forms of Jewish mysticism usually are considered to be *Ma'ascey Bereshit,* which means the study of the hidden doctrines of creation; and *Ma'ascey Merkavah,* or the study of the acts of the divine chariot, reflecting an expansion of Ezekiel's vision of the divine chariot. Actually they are represented in such earlier manuscripts as the *Shiur Komah,* which is the measurement of the divine body, or height; and in the *Hekhalot* literature, the study of the divine castle or inner sanctum of the Deity. These are apparently the earliest examples of the

---

* *exegesis*—an explanation or exposition, especially of the Scriptures.

mystical literature that has come down to us from post-Biblical times.

In the earliest forms of Jewish mysticism, knowledge was to a great extent based on a visual experience. The Song of Songs was construed as a mystical ecstatic dialogue of love between God and the people of Israel, a love expressed in visual sensual fantasy.

The study of these bodies of literature and of these doctrines was presumably reserved for the elect and for those whose piety was unquestioned, who would not be shaken by the penetration of these mysteries. That such mysteries have their dangers in antinomian consequences is well attested by specific incidents recounted in Talmudic literature.

From the Talmud, we obtain some hints of gnostic speculation. While literally *gnosis* means knowledge, Gnosticism is reflected in the Talmud in the use of certain symbolic or characteristic phrases which we know from Gnostic literature of the Hellenistic world. In non-Jewish Gnostic literature, mysticism represented a knowledge of the primeval struggle between the root principles or forces of good and evil. Open confession of such a dualism was of course taboo within a monotheistic culture. Nevertheless, we find hints of such dualisms, even in the Bible and in later philosophic literature.

Around the eighth century, Jewish mysticism began to take the form of a speculative cosmology based on the alphabet. The Hebrew alphabet was construed as the instrument of the Divine Creation, and the alphabet therefore could be used by the pious Jew to penetrate the mystery of creation. Once again we see that Jewish mysticism is a cognitive discipline.

Jewish mysticism is distinguished from Christian mysticism in that the Jewish mystic is prohibited openly from claiming any kind of union or identification with God or with the Godhead. There is always a chasm separating the Jewish mystic from the Deity Himself.

In medieval literature the tendency of Jewish mysticism was increasingly toward theoretical and theosophical speculation* based on the study of Scripture in which the words and letters of Scripture were presumed to be shells containing hidden secrets which could be known by the elect. The *Zohar,* or Book of Splendor, of the latter part of the thirteenth century, followed upon the *Bahir,* the Book of Light, of the twelfth century. All these traditions represent illumination; that is to say, they enable the pious man to penetrate through the darkness that separates man from God by an understanding of Scripture and of the essence of creation.

The various bodies of Jewish mystical literature present different points of view. The *Bahir,* for example, the earliest book of mysticism of medieval Europe, from Provence, contains some Gnostic doctrines which are clearly derived from ancient mythology; nevertheless, the attempt is always at cognition or knowledge. The visual element becomes clearly attenuated in medieval literature.

A major turn in Jewish mysticism occurred some time after the Expulsion from Spain in 1492, when a new form of Jewish Gnosticism came into being in Safed of Palestine in the middle of the sixteenth century. Here Jewish mysticism becomes not merely a body of knowledge of God and his secrets, but an understanding of God, that is to say, the condition of God's weakness in the universe. A totally new, mythologically oriented cosmogony was fabricated by the mystics of Safed, in which the process of creation was explained as a process of the withdrawal of God into himself, *tzimtzum.* The divine withdrawal resulted in a cosmic accident in which the divine vessels were broken, *sh'virat ha-kelim,* and the divine sparks were captured by the *sitra achrah,* or the nether world of evil. It is the function of man, specifically of

---

* *theosophical speculation* refers to a system of speculation which bases the knowledge of nature upon that of divine nature.

the pious Jew, whose suffering reflects the exile of God, to help in recapturing these sparks and in restoring them to their unity.

Hence, Jewish messianism, which in ancient terms had been interpreted as a nationalist redemption in the flesh, to return to the holy soil of the Holy Land, was in the sixteenth century represented as a cosmic drama in which the Jew participates; and through the performance of the *mitzvot* (religious obligations) he enables God to be restored to His original unity. When the final process of redemption of the Godhead will be achieved—when all the divine sparks will be retrieved—the cosmos and Israel will be reconstructed. Israel thus represents merely the consummation of the divine creation. This theory of mysticism introduced the doctrine of progress, so that with each new achievement in knowledge and good deeds there is progress in the process of divine redemption.

That mysticism occasionally had its aberrant forms is clear from the post-Sabbatian literature of adherents of Sabbatai Zevi, the pseudo-messiah who converted to Islam. This defection from Judaism plunged Jewish circles into such great despair that Nathan of Gaza and the followers of Sabbatai Zevi developed a mystical theology to explain gnostically how Sabbatai Zevi had had to convert in order to descend into the Pit and consume it so as to rid the world of its evil. Sabbatai Zevi's doctrine led directly to the movement organized by Jacob Frank, in which evil was made a form of mystical experience, and the very process of the enjoyment of the most taboo form of sin was regarded as part of the process of purging the world or bringing about a catharsis cleansing the world.

In the eighteenth century, following the debacle of Sabbatai Zevi and the thoroughly antinomian mystical movement of his followers (represented among others, by Jacob Frank), the Lurianic Kabbalah of Safed—the doctrine taught by Isaac Luria, known as the Ari—was popularized by Israel Baal Shem Tov and his followers into Hassidism. The major difference between Lurianic Kabbalah and Hassidism is that while Lurianic Kabbalah was reserved for the elect, the learned and the absolutely pious, in Hassidism every person from the most lowly to the most exalted participates in this doctrine of redemption. Every act is capable of restoring some spark of the Divine.

Sociologically, Hassidism represented an attempt to overcome the feeling of abject evil and of abandonment in which the Jews found themselves in the middle of the eighteenth century. Israel Baal Shem Tov indicated that, through joy and fervent prayer and song, even the most ignorant and most lowly could participate in the process of redemption. Thus, Hassidism, while often represented as a pietistic movement of ritual, was in its origins basically anti-elitist, for it pitted itself against the learned and held that even the most lowly strata of society could participate in the mystical process of redemption of God and of Israel.

These later forms of mysticism represented man as a participant in the divine drama. Hence, following the fifteenth century, one might say that Jewish mysticism had become far more active than cognitive and theosophical.

For Further Reading

Scholem, Gershom G. MAJOR TRENDS IN JEWISH MYSTICISM (New York: Schocken Books, 1941; paperback ed, 1961).

4

CHRISTIAN MYSTICISM

Mysticism has always existed within Christianity, but its persistence there, as in Judaism and Islam, has been ambiguous. An established religion flowing from the claims of divine revelation cannot be fully assimilated into the special experiences of any one of its adherents or a group of them. The principal body stands apart, secure in the hegemony of traditional belief, sometimes awed by the evidences of the mystics, but often censorious of what looks like mere enthusiasm. The purposes of organized religion are multifarious, but providing unmediated awareness of the "divine milieu" (to use Teilhard's phrase) is a minor one, if not one to be dismissed altogether.

Origins of Christian Mysticism

Nevertheless, the disposition of Christianity to mysticism was evident from its beginning. Another way of putting it is to point to the protracted influence of the earliest Christian language and the earliest Christian memories on reports of mystical experience taking place over the two thousand years of Christianity. While many ideas that originated later have been accorded orthodox status retrospectively, others seem to have a direct affiliation with the earliest Christian records. The Gospel according to St. John is steeped in the language of spirituality and illumination, and certainly it qualifies as a mystical document, even though many modern writers have been at pains to get beneath this level to something closer to the synoptic gospels.* The letters of St. Paul, perhaps the earliest Christian documents of all, contain evidence of Christian mystical experience as well as a well-developed warning against the extravagancies of mysticism.

Rufus M. Jones[1] in a classical study of the subject saw the mystical elements as intrinsic to Christianity's very being, and to the essential teachings of its central figure, Jesus Christ. The recorded sayings and actions of Jesus explicitly declare his personal experience of the real presence of God; the faith in Jesus himself that developed during and after his earthly lifetime calls for a persistent search by his followers after the same experience. Much depends on how mystical religion is distinguished from religion in general, and here with particular reference to Christianity. The isolating, esoteric element in mysticism which invokes official discouragement appears only at the ends of the mystical spectrum, although it has been made most visible because it has provided subject-matter for writers of genius. By this externalization of their experience through their writings, these men have opened the way for others, less gifted but of similar psychic organization, to make use of their experiences, and so to some extent have overcome the barriers of isolation.

Jones[1] saw in the personalities of individual mystics, and also in the development of mystical sects, efforts toward the recovery of a hitherto lost immediacy in religion. When traditional religious practices satisfy men deeply enough, no one needs to strike out on his own. The inevitable tendency of all institutions to become stylized, repetitious and insensitive, and to identify with the power of constituted authority has been evident within the Christian churches just as in secular organizations. And since, according to this way of thinking,

---

* *synoptic gospels* refers to the gospels which give accounts of the same events from the point of view of the observer, that is, the gospel according to Matthew, Mark or Luke.

there are always individuals who turn to religion for their spiritual growth, religious enterprises will emerge from time to time which try to bypass organized religion.

At the same time that a struggle must take place between the cohesive tendency in organized religion and the divisive tendency in mystical experience, so a parallel struggle takes place between the rigorously organized position and the highly individualized one of the mystics. *Heresy*, after all, means "choosing for oneself," and whoever claims to know the divine out of his own private devotions may be accused of "choosing" no less than nonmystical innovators who have fallen under the ban of orthodoxy. The "heretical" tendency in mysticism, with its occasional claims to transcend religious morality, as well as religious cognition, carries social and ethical consequences. Mysticism, then, shows in more than one of its orbits and throughout its history in the Christian world a tendency to be at odds with traditional religious belief and practice.

St. Ignatius of Loyola, founder of the Society of Jesus, was an extraordinary mystic whose initial seeming departure from traditional religion succeeded eventually in transforming the seat of power itself. Because of the intense activism associated with the Jesuits, Ignatius is not often recognized as a mystic. Yet he is not at all uncharacteristic of Christian mystics. Like him, as the founders of great orders still operating in the world, were St. Benedict and St. Francis. Though strikingly different in their lives and teachings, both of the latter based their contributions to the religious life on personal revelations of the divine being, which put them squarely within mystical traditions. They are all to be contrasted with the Dominican Prior of Erfurt, Meister Eckhart, who stands as perhaps the greatest of all Christian expositors of mystical speculative thought, but whose official ecclesiastical condemnation still holds. Eckhart does not appear to have been subversive of authority in any way except in his radical and stubborn affirmation of union with the Godhead, which, he taught, was a possibility for all Christians. Nor did Eckhart's mystical experience undermine his administrative powers, so far as we know.

The deepest roots of Christian mysticism go back to the New Testament itself. So, too, the deepest roots of the struggle between mysticism and authority in the Church probably also originate in the earliest Christian community, where all sorts of particularistic tendencies challenged the catholic unity of the growing world-household of believers. At bottom is the universal human problem of the individual and his group, or groups. But special aspects of this problem could be seen in the Christian teaching itself. For one thing, a faith that professes the continuing operation of a self-disclosing God as Holy Spirit, already manifested in the original Pentecostal event narrated in the Acts of the Apostles, is open to further self-disclosures through human agencies. Quite early in the life of the Church an extreme development of the doctrine of the Holy Spirit which fired the second century movement named for its founder as "Montanism" was accorded the support of the leading Church Father of the time, Tertullian. Montanus was an ecstatic mystic who interpreted his experience as evidence of the total self-disclosure of the Holy Spirit then and there, and his followers were encouraged to deviate widely from what had already become the traditions of Christian faith and practice.

This kind of group experience, based on the idea of an immediate apprehension of God, has appeared recurrently in Christianity, taking the most widely discrepant forms, from Montanism on the one hand to Quakerism on the other. Ecstatic elements in Quakerism, which were no less prominent to begin with, yielded early in its history to a predominance of disciplined inwardness, moral conservatism, and philanthropy of the broadest sort. In Quakerism the original high estimate of personal experience has not led to ascetical disciplines or to overtly "enthusiastic" mystical activity. The radical antinomianism of mystical sects might be seen reflected in Quaker opposition to military service, but as a matter of fact it has at times been honored more in principle than in Quaker practice.

That there should be a Christian mystical tradition is an apparent contradiction in terms, if we recognize in mysticism an individualistic and even aberrant form of religious experience within Christianity. One might expect rather that major mystical upheavals would each be paradigmatic and all be mutually exclusive. Nonetheless, such traditions do exist, and within them continuities of experience have lasted for centuries.

Dom David Knowles has illustrated one such tradition, the English, tracing it down to the seventeenth century from its origins in the middle ages.[2] It is significant that Knowles's examples of mystics were devoutly orthodox men and women in unquestioned communion with the Roman Catholic Church. Richard Rolle, Walter Hilton, Margery Kempe and Lady Julian of Norwich, as well as the anonymous author of "The Cloud Of Unknowing" and many others, were links in a continuous chain of mystical tradition. Personal experience, direct illumination, and access to the presence of God were part of the lives of all of them. Nevertheless they were all influenced by their predecessors and they submitted their personal enlightenment to the judgment of ecclesiastical authority.

Other traditions, while conforming to the canon law, may have contributed to the ultimate breakdown of Catholic unity in Europe. Their adherents founded separate communities and they encouraged individual and often eccentric private spirituality. The tradition of the Rhineland mystics and their communities may have facilitated the subversion of Papal authority by their profound engagement with the "spark" in the individual soul and perhaps also through their appeal to the masses, who were growing increasingly restive under Church authority.[3] But subversion of authority was not a major or even a conscious thrust of any Christian mystical tradition during the middle ages, when obedience to the Church was questioned for reasons quite different from those of immediate awareness of the divine ground and purpose.

It is thus possible to see more than one clear tendency in Christian mysticism, and each one has its meaning for the trends in mystical life today. One tradition of a very high order of philosophic thought stemmed from the experience and writings of the mysterious pseudo-Dionysius, who lived around the year 500 and whose ideas are themselves a Christian mystical distillate of a much older neo-Platonic tradition. His successors, all emphasizing the kind of ascetic theology which may be taken as a normative statement of the stages of mystical development, would include such disparate figures as Richard of St. Victor in Paris, Meister Eckhart and John Tauler in the Rhineland, and St. John of the Cross and St. Teresa of Avila in Spain. John's ASCENT OF MOUNT CARMEL is a classic sixteenth century statement of the progress of the contemplative soul to union with God, and his wonderful poems are an attempt at an existential statement of that progress.

Nor is that tradition extinct even now: Manuals of devotional practice within orthodox Christianity still define and prescribe the stages of interior prayer leading to enlightenment in ways derived from the tradition of the pseudo-Dionysius and his medieval lineage. Emphasizing as it does the attainment of unusual states of consciousness, this tradition parallels, and in some modern mystics like Thomas Merton becomes confluent with, Oriental traditions. It is noteworthy, too, that some of its language has been appropriated by exponents of psychedelic mysticism, among them Aldous Huxley. This raises the question, can the long and arduous "journey of the mind to God"—to use the title of St. Bonaventure's work—really be shortened by the introduction of a small amount of a powerful drug into the bloodstream?

Protestant Mysticism

While mysticism has been more at home in Eastern Orthodox Christianity than in the Western Catholic tradition, brief reference should be made to Protestant mysticism, as exemplified by Quakerism. There is no Protestant mystical tradition that corresponds to the traditions within Roman Catholicism. Jakob Boehme, the learned seventeenth century cobbler, propounded the mystical doctrine of the revelation of God throughout and within His creation.[4] Gnostic, alchemical and pantheistic elements pervade Boehme's teachings. It is a mysticism of "significances" influenced by the ideas of Paracelsus the physician. Emanuel Swedenborg, a true mystical seer, inaugurated a church on the foundation of his visions which continues quietly down to the present. Along with Boehme, Swedenborg was an important influence on the greatest of the mystical English poets, William Blake, but we do not see other than a very sporadic line of followers.

Boehme's highly intellectual speculations have been unwittingly parodied many times by earnest dabblers in esotericism who have extracted their own significance from the rich mines of the Bible and the natural sciences. It is hard to catch any characteristically Protestant note in this sort of latter-day gnostic mysticism, beyond the extreme and usually idiosyncratic individualism of its proponents. With the rise of modern skepticism, much of the quality if not the content of Protestant esotericism has passed into Nature mysticism. The original flinty specificity has been honed down to philosophical, optimistic, and not very rigorous pantheism.

Whether the larger part of Protestant "enthusiasm," past and present, is to be called mystical or not is moot. Biblical-literalist and pentecostal sectarianism have repeatedly given rise to outbursts of special forms of spirituality. Groups such as "the Jesus People" and practices like glossolalia are recent American examples. It would be difficult to detect the kinships that might exist between them and either the gnostic or the theological types of mysticism which have composed the main developments in Christianity. However, there is no doubt that the protagonists of these religious trends claim direct, unmediated divine inspiration no less than do the intellectually more impressive mystics.

References

1. Rufus M. Jones. STUDIES IN MYSTICAL RELIGION (London: Macmillan, 1909).
2. David Knowles. THE ENGLISH MYSTICAL TRADITION (London: Burns & Oates, 1961).
3. Rufus M. Jones. THE FLOWERING OF MYSTICISM (New York: Macmillan, 1939).
4. Jakob Boehme. THE SIGNATURE OF ALL THINGS (New York: E. P. Dutton, 1934) Everyman's Library ed.

5

HINDU MYSTICISM AS REPRESENTED BY SHRI RAMAKRISHNA

Psychological examination of the mystical experiences of a person remote from us in culture and tradition requires special prudence. Categorical differences existing between us in our origins and personal experiences must be taken into account in studying any person, mystic or not. In the case of really exotic cultural differences, allowance must be made for linguistic, social and all the other cultural idiosyncracies normally ignored when they are relatively slight. It is just such allowances that naïve Western observers of the Indian scene had trouble in making; at their crudest, they were those nineteenth century Christians for whom Victorian morality and theology, and behind that the whole Judeo-Christian conception of monotheism as opposed to polytheism, stood as objective reality. Confronted by such common symbols as the representation of the divine activity in sexual form and bewildered by the profusion of deities in the Hindu pantheon, they could impute to Hinduism a "decadence" following from its essence, and they failed to apply to that religion the discrimination between enlightened and superstitious observance which they would be sure to demand for their own.

Inadequate knowledge of the background of unfamiliar religious statements may also constitute a source of difficulty. Here is a religious world other than that of Abraham, Isaac and Jacob—a world that knows no Decalogue, no embattled and suffering people of God, no mystery of unique Incarnation and Resurrection, no Universal Church outside which there is no salvation. Reformations have taken place in that world, the blood of infidels has been shed, and there have even been attempts at updating it, but it is a different world.

The claim is sometimes made that within the specific religious field of mysticism, cultural differences do not hold sway. According to this version of the "perennial philosophy," mystical experiences have much more in common than they have dissimilarities proceeding from radically dissimilar traditions.[1] This seeming consonance of mystic experience depends to some degree on how one defines mysticism.

Shri Ramakrishna was one of the great mystics of all time, and the preeminent mystical figure of nineteenth century India. Inevitably we ask in the presence of such individuals how great is their own real contribution, and how great the importance of their followers through whose devotion, writings, and institutions the memory of the founders is not only preserved but also glorified. In the long run we have to satisfy ourselves with the reflection that something must lie behind the ardor of a great discipleship and look critically at the literature on our subject to try to get a clearer picture of the person as he presented himself. The final test of religious authenticity remains subjective: How do I now respond to the person as I reconstruct his presence? It is easy to understand why mystical figures are needed by people who cannot be satisfied with derivative experiences and require the presence of a new incarnation to convince them.

Shri Ramakrishna is the religious name—plus the honorific—of the second son of a poor Bengali Brahmin farmer. He was born in 1836 and died in 1886. Biographies of Ramakrishna abound in legends, some miraculous, some retrospectively premonitory of his sainthood. It is impossible to disentangle elements of historical fact in such narratives from the imaginative renderings of them which often sound like the legends surrounding the lives of others to whom divinity has been ascribed. It is important to bear in mind that the divinity of Ramakrishna as an incarnation of the Absolute, of God (however God is imagined or conceptualized), is accepted by a body of his followers. His own attitude toward this knotty problem of identity is somewhat comparable to the way in which the Gospel of Mark at certain junctures makes oblique allusions to the messianic mission of Jesus, at others gently dismisses the whole claim.

In addition to the biographical accounts of Ramakrishna there exists an extraordinarily revealing document, the large volume published by the Ramakrishna-Vivekananda Center under the title, THE GOSPEL OF SHRI RAMAKRISHNA.[2] For a period of four years, the last years of the life of the saint, a disciple not yet fully committed to the master lived intermittently at the temple compound at Dakshineswar, near Calcutta, taking down verbatim (most likely as recalled a short time afterward) conversations between Ramakrishna and persons around him—disciples, associates, pilgrims. The writer, Mahanendra Nath Dutt, who effaced himself on the title page under the mere initial M, later became a devotee of Ramakrishna, but only occasional remarks in his book invite the suspicion of editorial hindsight. The whole work was translated into convincing English by Swami Nikhilananda, whose biography of Ramakrishna, which precedes M's record, is notably free of crude hagiolatry.* A biography by Christopher Isherwood, RAMAKRISHNA AND HIS DISCIPLES,[3] is as charmingly written as one would expect of that author, but in it almost no effort is made to discriminate fact from legend.

While M's biography covers only four years of Ramakrish-

* *hagiolatry*—the worship of saints.

na's fifty, it contains many references to the master's earlier experiences, to which at least qualified belief may be given by the sympathetic but unconvinced reader. The verbatim record itself reports a large number of incidents of mystical states. These incidents are reported briefly as objective events, frequently with the simple statement, "The master passed into samadhi when he heard these words," but sometimes when Ramakrishna descended from this ecstatic state he could describe what had happened to him.

Ramakrishna's parents became themselves the focus of pious legends, not the least being the vision in anticipation of his mother's conception of him, in which the divinity of the boy was foretold. In bald fact, he was the third child and second son of his parents. His early childhood was remarkable only for his precocious learning. At six or seven he reacted to the sight of a flight of cranes coming out of a thunder cloud by falling to the ground unconscious. As recorded by Nikhilananda, this episode appears to have taken place shortly before his father's death, when he was seven. His attachment to holy men and to the traditional Hindu teachings was increased at that time, and it was not long before he began his training in meditation.

Later a rather remarkable episode occurred. Acting the part of the god Siva in a play, Ramakrishna became so lost in meditation and evidently so totally identified with the god that the performance as such ceased to be, and turned into a mystical experience. It seems clear that the frequency, intensity and profundity of his trances were impressive even in Hindu India, where such states are not rare. Ramakrishna's elder brother became a priest in a temple newly established near Calcutta, and later Ramakrishna himself became the priest at the shrine of Radhakanta, graced by the images of Radha and Krishna, who together symbolize union with God in ecstatic love.

Ramakrishna appears to have distinguished himself very

early from the run of Hindu priests by his persistence in taking seriously the inner meaning of rites which for them had become formalities. On his brother's death he succeeded him as the priest of Kali, the divine mother, who is represented with a severed head and a bloody saber, as well as offering gifts to her children. Ramakrishna turned to Kali with his usual fervor, protesting a longing for full consciousness of her presence. Just at the point when he was in such desperation that he thought of killing himself with her sword, he encountered an experience of her presence which was so overwhelming that, in his constant communion with her, he was believed to have become insane. A whole series of incidents of extraordinary behavior followed, in many of which he adopted mannerisms attributed to the god of his current devotion or of one of the god's traditional retainers, among them the monkey Hanuman.

At 23, Ramakrishna was married to a little girl of five, with whom he lived much later, although without ever engaging in sexual relations. He had another long period of apparent mental illness, marked by insomnia, weeping, and hallucinatory experiences, as well as his accustomed trance states. Later, when he was already regarded by many as an incarnation of God, he found a new spiritual identity as the woman Radha, the principal lover of Krishna. Once again the extremity of his identification, as that of a wildly lovesick girl, seemed to some of those around him as the mark of psychosis, although it is always difficult to believe in reading the account that the term psychosis, with its exclusively secular connotations, would be acceptable to those who saw in the supposed illness itself a mark of the man's spiritual development.

Later on, Ramakrishna was surrounded by a band of disciples who not only shared in many of his experiences but who founded an order which still exists, one known chiefly for its humanitarian efforts in India, and which is influential in the

Western world through its missions in behalf of Vedanta, the teaching of the Hindu Scriptures. Quite Indian in its own way, and yet marked by the enormous intensity of Ramakrishna's spirituality, was his transitory identification as Moslem and as Christian, when he had made himself familiar with these other revelations of the divine.

Some incidents from THE GOSPEL OF SHRI RAMAKRISHNA will give evidence of the kind of experiences related by Ramakrishna in direct quotation to his follower M. Most of these incidents have to do with the mystical experience par excellence—samadhi.

"It is the complete merging of the mind in God-consciousness," he is quoted by M as saying. Ramakrishna then distinguishes the samadhi in which there is no trace of the "I" left from that in which the "I" remains, the samadhi of the Lover and the Beloved. In this latter devotion, God allows the devotee to keep a little of "I" even after giving him the knowledge of Brahman so that he may realize he is enjoying the play of God. Ramakrishna recommended to a disciple that he give up his "ego." The man protested that he would have to give up the organization under his administration. Ramakrishna then differentiated again between the unripe or "wicked" ego, which needs to be abandoned, and the ripe or "child's" or "servant's" ego, which is the ego of knowledge.

Ramakrishna made it plain that in the highest state of samadhi there is no trace of the ego left. The loss is temporary, this state being like singing one's highest note, which cannot be indefinitely prolonged. On the other hand, in certain spiritual states Ramakrishna felt the need of another person's presence. At one time, he said with his usual candor, he turned to his own genitals as the representative of the divine phallus at the center of his worship, although he referred to this state as divine madness. In true higher samadhi, the aspirant loses all consciousness of the outer world and does not retain the physical body in his experience: "If milk is poured in his mouth it runs out again." In order to convey the holy teachings to others, however, men must come out of the samadhi state.

In a state of partial recovery from samadhi, Ramakrishna once was heard to say to the Divine Mother, "Please do come down, don't torment me this way. Be still, Mother, and sit down," whereupon he regained consciousness. He did not recommend teaching disciples the higher spiritual states at too early a stage in their development. He was quite capable of telling "naughty" jokes to young followers, explaining that even a vegetarian diet needs to be interrupted with "a little water smelling of fish."

Although no one could doubt the seriousness of Ramakrishna's faith or his sincerity, he also displayed a childlike simplicity of behavior and a total lack of self-reflectiveness. All sorts of seemingly trivial incidents served to put him immediately into a state of trance. On one occasion he was taken by his friends to Calcutta to watch a balloon ascend from the maidan there. He noticed a young English boy leaning against a tree and at the sight went into samadhi. His own explanation is simple and concise: The boy's body was "bent in three places"; Ramakrishna imagined the figure of Krishna in such a pose and this identification released the state of trance. On other occasions there was no explanation—a song, a passage in a play, anything could bring about the state of ecstasy, of union with God.

Speculation on the psychological meaning of Shri Ramakrishna's ecstatic states may come down to merely substituting psychological terms for his religious terms unless it seeks to provide some explanation of the dynamic condition underlying them. It is no guess to infer from the documentary evidence that altered states of consciousness occurred in which the saint appeared to be wholly out of contact with the world outside himself. Their resemblance to hypnotic cataleptic* states, hysterical or epileptic absences, and schizophrenic withdrawal is apparent. But there is no reason to hold to one of these diagnostic categories more than to another.

Despite the fact that Shri Ramakrishna was declared to be insane by some members of his family and some of his friends at one time in his career, the further inference that his later experiences were only psychotic manifestations or restitutions cannot be made, if indeed such claims can ever be made about anyone. His capacity to undergo instant identifications which could persist for long or short periods is characteristic of both schizophrenics and some hysterics. The record suggests, however, that his emergence from these identificatory states was not only unscarred but actually one of a deepening and enrichment of his ego. He was in his identification with Kali, or Krishna, or at another period, Christ, like a good traveler who assumes to himself whatever he finds thoroughly congenial in a foreign country and divests himself of the rest when he leaves.

That is not to say that the basic structure of Ramakrishna's personality was independent of neurotic organization. The capacity to split off parts of experience totally for the period of ecstasy and exalted identification so that he was for the time being no longer the person whose objective history outsiders knew, together with his evident isolation from persistent erotic ties at the human level with ordinary mortals, do suggest a schizoid form of personality. Even his concern for others appears to the reader of the record as a deeply narcissistic one in which the welfare of these others could not be a constitutive element. Everything points to Ramakrishna's ideal self as the focus of attention.

The definitive processes at work in forming this extraordi-

---

* *catalepsy*—a condition characterized by a waxy rigidity of the muscles, so that the patient tends to remain in any position in which he is placed.

nary man's personality can only be tentatively imagined, and when the language of psychopathology is employed, it may serve more as analogy than for legitimate diagnostic purposes. Again, cultural symbolic variations make themselves known, among other ways, by the selection of specific modalities of neurotic development. It would take us too far afield to dwell on this fascinating subject, but, for example, the Hindu preoccupation with Kali, the Divine Mother who both kills and creates, although finding its counterparts in Western unconscious images, must elicit varieties of castration anxiety peculiar to Indian culture. Modes of defense must be characteristically favored by the cultural setting: An environment that highly values the radical differentiation of the world of appearance from the world of existence must favor splitting. But a singularly strong personal predisposition is essential to turn these cultural predilections to effective account.

References

1. Aldous Huxley. THE PERENNIAL PHILOSOPHY (New York: Harper & Brothers, 1944).
2. Shri Ramakrishna. THE GOSPEL OF SHRI RAMAKRISHNA. Translated by Swami Nikhilananda (New York: Ramakrishna-Vivekananda Center, 1942).
3. Christopher Isherwood. RAMAKRISHNA AND HIS DISCIPLES (New York: Simon & Schuster, 1965).

6

JACOB FRANK AND THE FRANKISTS

The Frankist movement came into being among the Jews of Poland in the middle of the eighteenth century. While Jacob Frank himself was not a mystic, the Frankists are of interest in the context of mysticism for several reasons. They represent a movement whose origins are particularly illustrative of those environmental influences that create the occasion for the formation of mystical groups. They also illustrate the special vulnerability of these groups to breakdown, and to manipulation by demagogues.

The Frankist movement is attributed to two causes: (1) the messianism which agitated the Jewish world after the appearance of Sabbatai Zevi, the pseudo-messiah from Smyrna, and which developed later into religious mysticism; and (2) the social and economic upheaval in the life of Polish Jewry. The spread of messianism (1660-70) occurred in the period following the killing of Jews in the days of Chmielnicki.* Hundreds of ruined communities awaited aid from heaven and were inclined to see in the Ukraine massacres the premessianic sufferings foretold and in Sabbatai Zevi the coming messiah. Zevi's fall and his conversion to Islam estranged him from many of his followers, but among a small minority of Jewish people, the belief in his mission persisted.

Having lost its political significance, messianism at the end

* Bogdan Chmielnicki, born about 1595, led the Cossacks in massacres of the Ukrainian Jews in 1648-49.

of the seventeenth century assumed a mystical coloring, and an open popular movement was transformed into a secret sectarian cult. In Poland, particularly in Podolia and Galicia, there were formed numerous societies of Sabbataians, known among the people as "Shebs." In expectation of the great messianic revolution, the members of these societies threw off the burden of Jewish formalism, discarding many religious laws and customs. The mystical cult of the Shebs incorporated the elements of both asceticism and sensuality: Some of its members did penance for their sins and subjected themselves to self-inflicted torture; others disregarded the strict rules of chastity, at times giving themselves over to unbridled sensuality. The Polish rabbis attempted the extermination of this heresy at the Assembly of Lemberg (1722) and elsewhere, but could not fully succeed.

Jacob Frank, actually Jacob Leibowitz, was born in Podolia in 1726. At his birth, his grandmother, the community astrologist, solemnly said: "Guard this child; raise him well, because through him something new has been brought to the world." His father, Judah Leib, after falling under suspicion as an adherent of Sabbataianism, was expelled from the community he had served as rabbi. He settled in Wallachia, where Jacob grew up in an atmosphere filled with mystical and messianic fancies, and marked by superstition and moral laxity. From his early youth he showed repugnance to Talmudic study, and remained an "ignoramus," as he later called himself, "a plain man." While living with his parents in Wallachia, he first worked as a clerk in a shop; afterward, in his thirteenth year, he went to Bucharest as servant to a wealthy Polish Jew. It seems that he had already accepted lying and cheating for beautiful things as a way of life. Later he boasted to his disciples that by the age of 13 he had deceived his father for a set of new clothes for travel.

Frank's employer took him to Turkey, where Frank established his independence and conducted a business in jewels,

furs and silks. He lived in Salonika and Smyrna, the centers
of the Sabbataian sect. Here he received the name Frank, or
Frenck, a designation applied by Turkish Jews to all Euro-
peans. He became fascinated with the idea of returning to
Poland and playing the role of prophet and leader among
the oppressed and disorganized. He maintained that the
successive messiahs were not visionaries or frauds, but the
incarnation of one and the same messianic soul. King David,
Elijah, Mohammed, Sabbatai Zevi—all were one and the
same intrinsic personality, merely assuming different bodily
presentation. Why shouldn't he himself be an incarnation of
the messiah?

Conditions were unusually favorable. Frank acquired
some wealth, and in 1752 at age 26 married a very beautiful
14-year-old girl of Nicopolis, whom he later apparently
utilized as a lure for adherents. Two sons were born—Joseph
in 1753, Jacob in 1755—and then a daughter Eve in 1761.
But by 1755 Frank had made his appearance in Podolia.
There, joining hands with the local Shebs, he began initiating
them into the doctrines he had imported from Turkey. The
sectarians arranged a secret meeting, at which the religious
mysteries, centering in the Sabbatai Trinity (God, the Messiah, and a female hypostasis* of God, the Shekinah) were
enunciated. Frank was evidently regarded as the second person of the Trinity and as a reincarnation of Sabbatai, being
designated as S.S. (Santor Senior), "the Holy Lord." By virtue of his being part of the godhead, "the Messiah" had the
power to accomplish miracles. His followers vouched for his
performance of such miracles and were so firmly convinced
of his divine nature that they addressed mystical prayers to
him in the language of the *Zohar*.

Out of the Podolians Frank organized a sect of his own,
whose adherents were named in his honor the Frankists.

---

* Hypostasis referred originally to the essence of the triune Godhead,
and later came to indicate a member of the Trinity.

Among other things, he taught the acquisition of wealth in deceitful ways, but it was his lust for power which dominated him to the exclusion of every other motive. It was these characteristics that made his personality so fascinating and at the same time so ignoble. There was a certain demonic grandeur to the man.

The Frankists adopted as their passion the destruction of rabbinic Judaism, declaring war on the Talmud. The *Zohar*, they believed, was opposed to the Talmud, and the *Zohar* alone contained the true Law of Moses. For this reason Frank's adherents called themselves Zoharists and Contra-Talmudists (Anti-Talmudists). With spite they did the very things which rabbinic Judaism strictly forbade, even with reference to marriage and the laws of morality. For example, during a fair held in Podolia, Frank and his followers, both men and women, had assembled in an inn to hold their mystical services. They sang hymns, exciting themselves to the point of ecstasy by dancing. Inquisitive outsiders who managed to catch a glimpse of the assembly, afterward related that the sectarians danced around a nude woman (who may possibly have represented the Shekinah, the third person of the Trinity). The Polish authorities were informed that a Turkish subject was exciting the people and propagating a new religion.

Frank, being a foreigner, was banished to Turkey, and his followers were delivered to a conference of rabbis. There they admitted to acts which were subversive, not only of Judaism but also of the fundamental principles of morality and chastity. The women in particular told of the sexual excesses in vogue among the sectarians, including nudity, adultery and incest—all justified by mystical speculations regarding God's will.

In consequence of this testimony, a decree of excommunication was pronounced against the Frankists in Brody (1756). None must intermarry with them; their sons and daughters were to be regarded as bastards; even those who were merely under suspicion of some connection with the sect must not be permitted to occupy any religious office or act as teachers. This formal ecclesiastical curse was repeated in several communities. The formula was printed and widely distributed and was to be read in synagogue each month. The sentence of excommunication contained one point of special interest—that no one under 30 was permitted to occupy himself with the Kabbalah, or to read the *Zohar* or any other mystical work.

The Frankists were turned over to the Inquisition. They declared before the tribunal of Bishop Dembowski that they were in reality almost Christians, since they believed in a Trinity. To prove their complete rupture with Judaism, they claimed that the Talmud inculcated the murder of Christians as a religious duty. The Frankists were released from prison, permitted to live with their beliefs, and the new sect thus changed roles, from that of the victim of persecution by the Talmudic Jews to that of the persecutor.

To drive their enemies to despair, the Frankists requested a disputation between themselves and the Talmudists. They offered to prove, on the one hand, that their dogma of the Trinity was based upon the Bible and *Zohar*, and on the other that the Talmud was an abomination. Bishop Dembowski rapidly convicted the Talmudists and had the Frankists, with the assistance of the police, make a search for copies of the Talmud in his bishopric. About a thousand copies were thrown into a pit and burned at the hand of the executioner.

The sudden death of Bishop Dembowski (1757) brought about a swift change. Persecution turned against the Frankists. Frank was brought back from Turkey, and he formulated a new plan to rid himself and his adherents of all opponents. At first, Frank dwelt upon his exalted mission and the divine revelations which had commanded him to follow in the footsteps of Sabbatai Zevi. Just as Sabbatai had been compelled to embrace the faith of Islam temporarily, so Frank and his adherents were predestined in his view to adopt the Christian religion as a disguise and stepping-stone to "the faith of the true Messiah." Upon Frank's advice, six Frankists presented themselves "in the name of all" to accept baptism. A second disputation at Lemberg (June 1759) found the Frankists maintaining that the *Zohar* taught the doctrine of the Trinity, and that one person of the deity had become flesh, which the Talmudists could not refute without offending the Christians.

Approximately a thousand Frankists, urged by the priests to accept baptism at last, still hesitated, and did so only upon the explicit command of Frank and in his presence. Frank himself made his appearance on this occasion amid great pomp, in gorgeous Turkish dress, seated in a carriage drawn by six horses and surrounded by guardsmen. Frank submitted to a preliminary baptism, desiring to complete the ceremony with greater solemnity in Warsaw. In 1759 he appeared in Warsaw and induced the king to act as his godfather.

The columns of the Warsaw newspapers were full of reports of the baptism of many Jews occurring daily and of the high noblemen and noble ladies who acted as godparents. Nevertheless, Frank was watched with suspicious eyes by the priests. They realized that he was an impostor who, under the guise of Christianity, sought to gain prominence for himself and his sect. His Polish adherents were secretly questioned about his doings, his past, and his aims. Several of them finally betrayed him, informing the ecclesiastical authorities that his acceptance of Christianity was a mere sham and that he was himself worshipped as Messiah, God and Holy Lord. He was arrested, examined by the officials of the Inquisition, and sent to the Fortress of Czestochova in 1760. Only the fact that the king was his godfather saved him from being burned at the stake as a heretic. Some of his followers were condemned to work in the trenches of the fortress, while others were ordered to return to their native places.

For 13 years (1760–1772) Frank remained in the citadel, but the Catholic clergy failed in its purpose. The Frankists continued their association with the "Holy Lord" who as a suffering messiah was now crowned in their eyes with a new halo. They even managed to penetrate the fortress itself, settling in large numbers on the outskirts of the town, which in accordance with old messianic notions, they designated as "the gates of Rome," the legendary dwelling place of the Messiah. They beheld in Frank's fate a repetition of the destiny of Sabbatai Zevi, who had also been kept prisoner—in the castle of Abydos, near the capital of Turkey. They were inspired by Frank's mystical discourses and epistles, the gist of which was that their only salvation lay in the "holy religion of Edom," a term by which he designated a strange mixture of Christian and Sabbataian ideas. The new religion was devoid of any truly religious or moral element, reflecting Frank's statement, "I have come to rid the world of all the laws and statutes which have been in existence hitherto."

The first partition of Poland put an end to Frank's imprisonment in the monastery, and he was released by the commander of the occupying Russian troops. After a brief stay in Warsaw, where he managed to reestablish direct relations with the sectarians, Frank left the boundaries of Poland accompanied by his family and a large retinue, settling in Brünn, Moravia (1773). There he lived until 1786, surrounded by numerous sectarians and "pilgrims" who came from Poland. For many of the pilgrims there was great attraction in the person of Eve, Frank's beautiful daughter, who at this time began to play an important role in the organization of the sect.

Frank's further exploits were performed in Western Europe. In Austria he assumed the role of Christian missionary to the Jews and even succeeded in gaining the favor of the Court in Vienna. However, his past soon became known, and he was firmly requested to leave Austria. Frank then settled in Germany, in Offenbach, where he presumptuously claimed the title, "Baron of Offenbach." In his new place of residence, Frank, assisted by Eve, the "Holy Lady," stood at the head of his circle of sectarians. There, supported by his Polish and Moravian partisans, he led a life of ease and luxury.

After the death of Frank, which occurred in 1791, his sect began to disintegrate and the flow of gifts for the benefit of the Offenbach Society gradually ceased. In the face of unsuccessful endeavors to attract sectarians, Eve, as Frank's successor, found herself entangled in debts. Pursued by her creditors, she died allegedly in 1817 at the age of 56, in Offenbach, although some maintain that she escaped. Never married, Eve was referred to always as a virgin, and, like her father, was accused of being a total swindler. Nevertheless she was surrounded with an air of mystery. Rumor had it that she was the foster daughter of Frank, that she was actually the child of the unmarried Elizabeth, daughter of Peter the Great.

The Frankists who had stayed in Poland, although outwardly Catholics, remained loyal to the "Holy Lord" down to the day of his death. For a long time they intermarried and were known in Poland under the name of the Neophytes. Gradually, however, they merged with the Catholic population, losing the character of a sect, completely absorbed at last by their Polish environment. Absorption thus followed a process in which visionary mysticism degenerated into mystification, and messianism into an endeavor to throw off the "Jewish sorrow" by renouncing Judaism.

For Further Reading

Arnsberg, Paul. VON PODOLIEN NACH OFFENBACH. DIE JÜDISCHE HEILSAR-. MEE DES JAKOB FRANK (ZUR GESCHICHTE DER FRANKISTISCHEN BE-WEGUNG). (Offenbach: Offenbacher Geschichtesverein, 1965).

Dubnow, Simon M. HISTORY OF THE JEWS IN RUSSIA AND POLAND, FROM EARLIEST TIMES UNTIL THE PRESENT DAYS. Translated by I. Friedlaender. (Philadelphia: Jewish Publication Society of America, 1916–20) 3 vols.

Graetz, Heinrich H. FRANK UND DIE FRANKISTEN, EINE SEKTENGESCHICHTE AUS DIE LETZTEN HÄLFTE DES VORIGEN JAHRHUNDERTES. (Breslau: Grass, Barth & Co., 1868).

Graetz, Heinrich H. HISTORY OF THE JEWS. Translated by Bella Löwy (c. 1891–98) (Philadelphia: Jewish Publication Society of America, 1956) 6 vols.

THE JEWISH ENCYCLOPEDIA. A descriptive record of the history, religion, literature, and the customs of the Jewish people from the earliest times to the present day; prepared under the direction of Cyrus Adler (and others), Isadore Singer, Managing Ed. (New York & London: Funk & Wagnalls, 1901–06) 12 vols.

Scholem, Gershom G. MAJOR TRENDS IN JEWISH MYSTICISM (New York: Shocken Books, 1946).

7

IGNATIUS LOYOLA AND THE SOCIETY OF JESUS

Inigo, or Ignatius Loyola, was born in 1491 at Loyola in Spanish Biscay. Little is known of his early years except that he was sent as page to Ferdinand and Isabella, and that later on, faithful to the traditions of his family, he became a soldier. According to his biographers, he was a handsome, graceful person who spent a great deal of time in looking as grand as his rather diminutive height would permit. A contemporary official document, a minute of a correctional court dated 1515, has preserved a description of the man. He is portrayed as being bold and defiant, clothed in leather trousers, armed with dagger and pistol, his long hair flowing from beneath his knight's cap; the judge further describes his character as cunning, violent and vindictive.

Ignatius' chief characteristic was a passionate love of glory and renown. He combined within himself great vanity, being a gambler, a dueler, and a casual lover, a man of intelligence and courage, exact in his performance of all his military duties. His military career was marked by only one experience under fire. In May 1521, in a rather foolhardy attempt at defending a city against overwhelming odds, Ignatius stood on the battlements, sword in hand, encouraging a small group of countrymen to resistance. He was struck in his left leg by a heavy stone dislodged from a wall at the same instant that a cannonball shattered his right leg. Ignatius was soon

after carried to his own home. His right leg had been clum-
sily set by a French surgeon, and it was necessary to break the
leg again in order to reset it. Again the bones knitted improp-
erly. One of them protruded below the knee, and such a
deformity was insupportable to this vain man. It would prevent him from ever again wearing the high, tight-fitting
boots of the smartly dressed officer. At his insistence, the
protruding bone was cut off. After this operation, it was
discovered that the wounded leg was considerably shorter
than the other because of a hip contracture. Ignatius had it
violently stretched by iron instruments—a surgical rack—but
after all this, he was still left with a slight, though noticeable,
limp.

Compulsory rest followed. Ignatius' only previous reading
had been stories of chivalry and romance, but all that could
be found now were the Flos Sanctorum (LIVES OF THE
SAINTS) and a Life of Jesus Christ by Ludolph the Carthu-
sian. Ignatius' attention became riveted to the message and
an impulse whispered to him to go and do as the saints had
done. On Our Lady's feast day she appeared to him as he lay
awake at night. No word was spoken, but Ignatius offered
himself to her, promising he would follow the standard of
Jesus Christ. Later he positively testified that from that moment, he never again gave the slightest consent to any im-
pure thought. He would settle for no middle course; no
ordinary life of holiness could satisfy him.

In order to place himself under the protection of Mary,
Ignatius made a solemn vow of chastity. He then traveled to
Manresa, where he stayed at the hospital. Wishing to rival the
saints in austerity and penance, he fasted on bread and
water, wore a hair shirt and an iron chain under his rags,
slept on the ground, and received corporal punishment
three times daily. He claimed all the most menial and repul-
sive tasks in the hospital. He begged, was beaten and in-
sulted. Finally he threw himself at the feet of his confessor
and admitted to an almost irresistible longing for suicide. But

it was here at Manresa that he thought out THE SPIRITUAL
EXERCISES,* and it was here that he expanded his need from
that of expiating his own past errors to that of an apostolic
zeal. He preached.

In Manresa, too, strange "illuminations" had already
begun to make their appearance. According to his own story,
Ignatius while walking along the bank of the river felt a
peculiar "condition," in that he was able to recognize many
things applying both to spiritual life and to faith. Everything
seemed suddenly new to him. It was a great "light of understanding," and he had the feeling that no natural experience
could at any time have taught him so much as this single
moment of divine knowledge. On the steps of the church of
Manresa he became aware of "a higher light," which showed
him how God had created the universe. Then he saw "the
Catholic dogma so clearly" that he was prepared to die for
the doctrine which he had seen in this manner.

One day there appeared to Ignatius "something white like
three keys of a clavichord or an organ." He was convinced
that this was the Holy Trinity. In the apparition of a white
body "not very large and not very small," he believed he
could see the person of Christ; in another, similar vision, the
Virgin Mary. Frequently he saw a great lighted sphere "a
little larger than the sun," which he explained as Jesus
Christ.[1]

In his newborn missionary role Ignatius resolved to devote
his life to the conversion of the infidels and schismatics of
Syria. On a pilgrimage to Jerusalem, he stopped first at
Barcelona, where he declined the use of bed and mattress.
He made holes in the soles of his shoes, penance for having
formerly been so proud of his military boots. He also discip-

---

* THE SPIRITUAL EXERCISES, according to Father de Ravignan, is "a man-
ual of Retreats, a method for meditation, and at the same time a collection
of thoughts and precepts for directing the soul in the work of interior
sanctification and in the choice of a state of life."

lined himself with a chain. He traveled from Barcelona to
Rome, to Venice, to Jaffa, and then to Jerusalem. The Fran-
ciscans, who exercised jurisdiction over the Christians in the
Holy Land, asked Ignatius to return to Europe, for appar-
ently his presence and behavior were only adding to the
Moslems' antipathy toward the Christian inhabitants.

In 1526 Ignatius proceeded to the University of Alcala to
follow a course in philosophy, and at that time began to give
the SPIRITUAL EXERCISES to those who came to consult him.
He was accused of heresy, examined by the Inquisitor, and
found to be innocent. However, as he was strongly advised to
leave Alcala, he moved on to the University of Salamanca. At
about this time two noble widows, a mother and daughter,
resolved to give up their fortune and position in his honor
and to spend their lives on pilgrimages. He was accused of
having induced them to take this rash step, for which he was
arrested and imprisoned. Because the two ladies publicly
testified that he had not encouraged them, he was released.
What few belongings he had he packed upon a burro and
left.

In 1528 Ignatius entered Paris, to take courses once again.
Here, as at Alcala and Salamanca, his austere mode of life,
his influence over the youth of the community, and the
popularity of his SPIRITUAL EXERCISES, which he continued to
give to many of his fellow-students, all excited suspicion and
jealousy. He was denounced to the tribunal of the Inquisition. Nothing reprehensible, however, could be found in his
conduct or doctrines.

Ignatius slowly gathered his six companions. He explained
to them the ends and the means of the order he was about to
found: Its end was to the greater glory of God and the
salvation of souls; and the means by which this end should be
attained were self-denial and works of charity and zeal. On
the Feast of the Assumption in 1534, the seven assembled in
a little chapel on Montmartre, where all made vows of pov-

erty and chastity. They bound themselves to labor in the Holy Land or, failing that, to offer themselves to the Pope.

The evils which Ignatius took up the task of combating were begging, unemployment, child neglect, and prostitution. To the prevention of the latter he devoted his most earnest attentions, announcing that he would give his life if only to prevent the sins of a single prostitute on a single night.

In 1537 Ignatius and two companions arrived in Rome to obtain permission from Paul III to receive Holy Orders. The time was ripe. Paul was opposing the storm of rebellion within the Church; Luther had broken his monastic vows, had proclaimed liberty of thought and rebellion, and was making gains; several German states and all of Switzerland had detached themselves from Rome; England was next; and Calvin's teaching was spreading fast through the southern provinces of Catholic France.

Paul III was sparing no efforts to stem the tide of revolt. Within this context Ignatius arrived in Rome, coming to the Pope in filial devotion with the solemn promise of poverty, chastity and obedience. The opinion has been voiced that the Jesuits were founded, by design, for the purpose of stemming the tide of the Reformation. Certainly it is true that the movement turned out to be one of the most formidable weapons in the armory of the Counter-Reformation. What can be said is that Ignatius Loyola appeared at the psychological moment, whether by accident or by design.

On Christmas night in 1538, Ignatius, who had previously deferred this event, said his first Mass. He then presented the plan and Constitution of his Institute to the Pope, who in September 1540 gave his solemn approval in the Bull "Regimini Militantes Ecclesiae." The Society of Jesus, founded six years before, was thus canonically established and recognized. Ignatius was elected General, and on Easter Sunday of 1541 he accepted the governorship of the Society.

While Ignatius remained in Rome, the members of the order dispersed, particularly directing their efforts toward obedience and self-sacrifice. Ignatius occupied himself with his novices in Rome, where he founded the monastery of St. Martha for fallen women; built two schools for orphans; and established a house of refuge for Jewish proselytes, in whose conversion he took a special interest. But his greatest works were the founding of the Roman College for the education of an elite clergy and, two years later, the Germanicum.

Except for his limp, which always remained, there was little to identify the General of the Society of Jesus with the knight of the past. Ignatius had become enfeebled by labor rather than by age, and so thoroughly had a constant habit of self-control subdued his enthusiasm that he was generally thought to be of a cold and distant disposition. For a long time he had suffered from an undiagnosed stomach ailment. Often the pain made him very weak, despite which he kept steadily at work. The intimate communications with divinity that were granted to him at Manresa continued throughout his life, and biographers tell of his long and frequent ecstasies, when he remained absorbed for hours in the "contemplation of God's infinite perfections."[2]

On July 31, 1556, Ignatius died; he was 65. He was beatified by Paul V in 1609 and canonized by Gregory XV in 1622. Because he had, after being elected General, kept himself so well out of sight, some surprise was expressed at the movement to canonize him. "Why!" exclaimed one Roman priest, "I always knew that he was a very good man, but I never thought of him as a saint."

References

1. René Fülöp-Miller. THE POWER AND THE SECRET OF THE JESUITS (New York: Viking Press, 1930) p 44.
2. B. N. THE JESUITS: THEIR FOUNDATION AND HISTORY (New York: Benziger Brothers, 1879) p 86.

For Further Reading

Brodrick, James S.J. SAINT IGNATIUS LOYOLA (New York: Farrar, Strauss & Cudahy, 1956).
———. THE ORIGIN OF THE JESUITS (New York: Longmans, Green, 1940).
Fülöp-Miller, René. THE POWER AND SECRET OF THE JESUITS (New York: Viking Press, 1930).
Hollis, Christopher. SAINT IGNATIUS (New York: Harper & Brothers, 1931).
B. N. THE JESUITS: THEIR FOUNDATION AND HISTORY (New York: Benziger Brothers, 1879).
O'Conor, J. F. X, S.J. THE AUTOBIOGRAPHY OF ST. IGNATIUS (New York: Benziger Brothers, 1900).
Renell, Sister M., S.S.N.D. IGNATIUS LOYOLA AND FRANCIS DE SALES (St. Louis: B. Herder, 1966).
Van Dyke, Paul. IGNATIUS LOYOLA (New York: Charles Scribner's Sons, 1926).
Young, William J., S.J. LETTERS OF ST. IGNATIUS OF LOYOLA (Chicago: Loyola University Press, 1959).

8

THE PSYCHOLOGICAL POINT OF VIEW

It is evident that the phenomena encompassed by and related to the term *mysticism* are numerous. They include states of mind of the individual, the nature of his relation to the world around him, and his behavior within the community in which he resides. It follows that a proper psychological account of mysticism which would do justice to all these differing aspects must be correspondingly subtle and complex. Yet these varied phenomena must share at least one property which warrants their being associated with the term *mysticism*. It is reasonable, therefore, to seek some common psychological mechanism at work in all of them.

THE MYSTICAL TRANCE STATE

The mystical trance state should be described first because, although the least common, it is nevertheless the most dramatic and probably the most extreme of those phenomena subsumed under the rubric of mysticism. In the trance state, the external world is excluded from consciousness more or less completely, or its impact is muted—attention is turned away from it. To the extent that the external world is perceived, the impressions of it are distorted. Visual sensations seem brighter or dimmer than their stimulus would warrant. Sounds seem louder or softer. Sensations arising in bodily functions may be magnified. For example, there may be intense awareness of the beating of one's heart or the throbbing of one's blood vessels or the sounds of one's breathing. Sensory experiences develop affective connotations. Inanimate objects seem threatening or kindly or ominous. Several of the modalities of sensation respond to a stimulus which ordinarily elicits the response of only one—a phenomenon known as synesthesia.

As the perception of the external world is suppressed, it may be replaced by hallucinatory experiences. These hallucinations may be formed or unformed. Unformed, they appear mostly in the visual sphere—occasionally in the auditory sphere. They are interpreted as water, mist, rocks or jewels. The appearance of scintillation is described frequently, as is a sense of the sound of whispering or blowing.

With respect to the formed hallucinations, there is no uniformity. They, also, are mostly visual, with only minor auditory components. The images are usually derived from the religious background of the individual. They may be described as "unnatural" or "supernatural." There may be figures of forms, buildings, rooms, mountains, forests, oceans—all of immense magnitude and incomparable brilliance.

Some subjective sensations are encountered frequently. The subject will usually say that his mystical experiences are "more real" than conventional reality. He experiences a sense of elevation in any of the meanings of that term. He may describe ecstatic feeling, or he may say that he feels literally transported to a high place such as a mountaintop. He will commonly declare that his experiences are indescribable in conventional language. He usually experiences some kind of contact or union with a divine being.

Anxiety may be felt at the outset of the experience, but when the mystical adventure succeeds, the anxiety is soon replaced by ecstasy. Sensations of familiarity, unfamiliarity or weirdness are often experienced, as well as the feeling of depersonalization, or "expansion of the self." Commonly the subject describes a sense of revelation, of new knowledge, of "seeing a light." In fact, he often speaks of "seeing the light" both figuratively and literally.

The mystical state, as described by those who experience it, reminds one of states of mind described under other circumstances. For example, the hallucinogenic drug experience resembles the mystical trance and, in fact, hallucinogenic drugs are used at times in rituals of an organized religion and at times individually to induce the mystical state. Such a drug-induced mystical experience seems to satisfy the criteria of some theologians for religious validity.

The onset of schizophrenia is often marked by a similar aversion to or detachment from the world of reality, with a complementary adversion to sensations arising intrapsychically. Many incipient schizophrenics feel that something bad has been rejected and a new and promising vision of life attained, after such an episode. Here, too, there is sensory distortion or hallucinatory replacement of sensation. This acute schizophrenic state seldom lasts more than a few moments, hours or days, ultimately giving way to one of the more enduring and familiar syndromes of the disorder.

In seizure states originating in the temporal lobe that are caused by organic disease, states of mind are encountered which are accompanied by the perceptual distortions, the hallucinations and the disturbances in the sense of reality, familiarity or both that are characteristic of the mystical state. The sense of ecstasy, expansion or elation is usually not experienced, although occasionally it may be.

The trance state may be considered to possess dynamic significance, whether induced by mystical preparation, by hallucinogenic drugs, or spontaneously, by an acute schizophrenic attack. Consciousness is occupied by intrapsychic sensations. This means that the external world has been removed from the individual's awareness and therefore seems to have been destroyed. The area of awareness usually occupied by the external world is now occupied by sensations which arise internally. These are illusorily interpreted as manifestations of the outside. The world of outer consensual reality, then, is replaced by the world of inner sensation, which *seems* to be the real world. The sense of reality is usually transferred from the outside inward with the permission of an indulgent ego which, to a certain extent, foregoes strict reality testing. The impression already referred to— that the outer world is destroyed—is complemented by an impression that it is being replaced by a new world—that the world is being reborn.

To a remarkable degree the form of the fantasy seems to be consistent, no matter how the trance state is induced, or in whom. The content can often be understood as the resolution of the problem which motivated the divorce from reality in the first place, whether it has come about as a result of psychic stress or as a result of deliberate rather than fortuitous intoxication. Usually the fantasy represents a reunion of some kind with the individual from whom the subject feels alienated. This reunion may take the form of an approach, an embrace, a sexual act, or a physical merging. The objects of the union often seem to be one or both parents, individually or together. Sometimes the parents are represented directly, sometimes by other humans, or sometimes—in a religious context—as God or other figures with supernatural or even divine attributes.

The affect which accompanies the experience is determined by a number of factors. It retains some residue of the distressing affect which prevailed before the trance began and which may have played a role in inducing the trance. Often anxiety is generated by the dissociation from the world of reality. The subject also feels the pleasure which follows the escape from the pressures of reality into a gratifying fantasy. Therefore in some instances panic or dread is encountered; in others, ecstasy; and in still others, a fluctuation between unpleasant and pleasant states.

We have no reliable data that would permit us to study the psychological occasion for mystical withdrawal. The acute schizophrenic detachment which resembles the mystical withdrawal is usually precipitated by some disappointment in relations with other individuals, whether that disappointment is initiated by the subject himself or by the person he loves. It seems likely that the difficulty of the mystic (who is generally not mentally ill), which brings about a withdrawal from the society in which he lives, may arise either in his relationship with another individual or in his relationship with his community. That is, there are circumstances when the demands the community imposes upon its members are so stringent that many cannot comply, and mystical detachment is a way of escaping those demands.

The term *community demands* applies to situations in which economic hardship or political oppression absorbs major portions of the individual's energy, leaving him little opportunity for gratification. However, it may be just as difficult for an individual to find himself in a society which, because it has been disrupted by war, revolution or disaster, fails to protect him and to provide him with that sense of belonging to a community which he requires. Here, too, there is a demand in the sense that the individual must do for himself what one ordinarily expects of the society in which he resides. We shall return to this discussion of the mystic in society.

Let us now consider the genesis of two aspects of the mystical trance—namely, the origin of the trance state itself and the origin of its contents.

Origin of the Trance State

The kind of psychic functioning which takes place in the trance state can be compared to what might be imagined to be the psychic functioning of an infant. In both cases the subject has no awareness of hard external reality which is not immediately relevant to himself. He gives his full attention to sensations arising within his body and within his mind, hallucinating the fulfillment of his needs. (This is the state which in psychoanalytic metapsychology is called primary narcissism.) Ordinarily the individual leaves this state behind as his perceptual capacities mature and as he acquires not only the images but the concepts of an outside reality with which he must contend. The readiness to revert to this primal state, while it may create vulnerability to mental illness, can be used defensively when external reality becomes too distressing. When this regression becomes obligatory to the extent that the subject cannot by an act of will prevent or reverse it, we consider him psychotic. When the regression proceeds to the point of transferring the sense of reality from outside inward while at the same time the regression can be voluntarily intensified or resisted or terminated, we see a trancelike state such as we have been describing. When the situation is clear-cut, diagnosis is not difficult. However, states of mind are sometimes encountered which do not fall cleanly into one category or the other.

Some individuals participate in every visible way in the real world, but nevertheless attribute personal meaning, not consensually shared by the larger society, to their images of the ordinary individuals and objects they encounter. In such individuals a residue of this primal state of mind flavors external reality and softens its impact.

Contents of the Trance State

What about the origin of the contents of the trance state? The creatures of the trance usually represent a deity. Sometimes there are two such figures, one male and one female, or a member of the divine court as it is given in the religious tradition of the subject. Often these creatures are seen in a closed or circumscribed space, or on a high place, approached from an open space or from below.

The action of the fantasy focuses on the relation between the subject and the representation of the deity. It may be that the subject only "sees" this supernatural figure, but in such instances it is implied that merely seeing him is itself a wondrous experience. Or the subject may also approach the deity. Something may be revealed or done to him by the deity, or he may unite with the deity. As he experiences this trance state, the subject feels himself illuminated, expanded or inspired, or as acquiring wisdom and power.

Both the ego state of the trance experience and its content strongly suggest that it is a regression to an infantile condition. The content of the trance fantasy symbolizes the gratification of desires to see the parent or parents, especially hidden and wondrous aspects; desires to approach, enter into, or experience some physical contact with the parent; or desires to unite and become one with the parent.

Incorporating this summary statement together with the considerations previously noted, we reach the following conclusion: Confronted with an unacceptable reality— intrapsychic, personal or social—the subject turns his back on that reality, excluding it from his consciousness and psychically destroying it. He replaces it with a new inner reality which he has so designed that it gratifies rather than frustrates him. This process represents a rebirth, a return to a state of mind characteristic of his infancy, when he was able to deal with frustration and disappointment by retreating to a world of fantasy and when he also enjoyed a firm and intimate union with his parents. Achieving this union once again in fantasy, he now feels vigorous and powerful, no longer dependent upon the whims of other people.

Those who experience the trance state usually speak of a feeling of invigoration and of power which appears during the trance and usually persists for some time thereafter. The feeling of being energized usually contrasts sharply with the feeling of dismal unhappiness and inertia which preceded the trance—sometimes referred to as "the dark night of the soul." It may be inferred that the detachment from frustrating reality has liberated the individual from the depressing and enervating influences of that reality. Both this freedom and the illusion of uniting with the omnipotent parent create the feeling of alertness, vitality and strength.

THE MYSTICAL WAY OF LIFE

While the trance with its drama creates the strongest impression, it constitutes only a small part of the mystical life. Among those individuals who do experience trances, these occur infrequently and last only a relatively brief period of time. The mystical life led by such individuals possesses its own qualities, even though these may be considered either as the preparation for or the consequence of the trance. Many, in fact, who regard themselves as leading a mystical life have never experienced a mystical trance. In some mystical movements the trance plays no role—for example, in Jewish mysticism, whether cabbalistic or hassidic. The emphasis in such cases is on the mystical way of life, not on the experience of dissociation.

The essence of the mystical life has been described as seeing the mundane things and people and events of everyday reality as the worldly representations of a supernal world, itself invisible to the eye of the unilluminated. Awareness of this supernal world makes it possible for the individual to appreciate the otherworldly significance of this-worldly objects.

Pursuing the psychological analysis, we might say that the mystic continues psychically to reside in the world of consensual reality in the sense of behaving appropriately and performing his role within the community. At the same time, to overcome the frustration and disappointment which seem to him to arise within the lower world, he looks for satisfaction in the experience of reverting to infantile narcissism—in feeling, if not in behavior. He reinterprets what he sees of the external world as a representation of the inner world, thereby making it possible to tolerate the external world. In a sense, the latter is made more palatable by being "flavored" by the inner world and its affects.

What the mystic does that is different from what his fellow citizens do depends upon the basis of his mysticism and upon the nature of his relationship to his community. Many of the important things done by the mystic he relates to the mystical experience. Some things he does to prepare for or to invite the experience, he says, and he does other things because he is influenced by it. From a superficial point of view, his explanation may be accepted. However, the activities which he claims are determined by the mystical experience may actually be motivated by unconscious needs, probably the same needs which invoke the trance. It does no violence to the facts to infer that his adoption of the mystical attitude and way of life performs an adaptive function by making it possible for him to cope with social stresses which threaten to overwhelm him.

In order to prepare for the mystical experience, individuals engage in activities which may be seen as methods of undoing sin, such as confession, abstinence, penitence or purification. These activities are sometimes encountered outside the religious context among individuals who are trying to ward off depression by consciously or unconsciously inviting the forgiveness, love and protection of a parental figure. In a few bizarre instances, an indulgence in "sin" prepares for the mystical experience. This indulgence in sinful behavior is seen as a means of purification. By descending to the depths of depravity, the subject "destroys the power of evil." The desperate pursuit of sensual gratification can be utilized also in the attempt to prevent depression because it replaces the emptiness of impending depression with the excitement provided by sensual experience.

Mystics may say that the mystical experience encourages them to commit themselves to a purer, that is, abstinent way of life. Such a commitment is sometimes seen as an attempt to prevent the return to depression after a period of relief and well-being.

To summarize, the mystical way of life, as exemplified in religious mysticism, contains two components: first, a minimizing of one's sensitivity to external reality and a complementary maximizing of sensitivity to inner "reality" by partial regression to primary narcissism; second, the deployment of one or more of the maneuvers commonly used to ward off depression.

Mystic vs Schizophrenic

While the mystic may seem to be following in the footsteps of the schizophrenic in retreating from outer reality to inner reality, he does not go all the way in his retreat. He differs from the schizophrenic in three important ways: First, his retreat is facultative rather than obligatory; second, it is partial rather than complete, as compared to the schizophrenic's retreat; third, he finds it possible, frequently desirable, to associate with others who share his view of the world—that is, he participates in mystical fraternities, while the schizophrenic rarely is able to form or maintain similar affectionate ties with others.

The "reality" from which the schizophrenic and the mystic retreat is often the reality of the demands of affectionate ties. The schizophrenic finds his difficulty either in emancipating himself from his parents early in life or in coming to terms with his spouse as an adult. The mystic finds the demands and constraints of the society in which he lives too difficult. In a sense, then, both the schizophrenic and the mystic retreat from social reality in two ways. On a personal psychological level, they withdraw interest from the world that presents itself to their senses. On a social level, they withdraw themselves from the society in which they live. They differ in that the schizophrenic can and does maintain this withdrawal by sustaining his regression from normal psychic function to infantile narcissism. The mystic's withdrawal to infantile narcissism is overwhelming for the brief trance periods during which they occur, and it is partial or not evident at most other times. He must often reinforce his withdrawal from the larger society by creating a small society which is held together by the common interests of its members.

Since it is the authority and the associated demands of the larger, older society which the individual mystic cannot accept, the new society must be democratic and fraternal, without an established hierarchy. In order to obviate the demand for intense, affectionate attachments, the new society usually requires abstinence and self-control. The mystical society thus deliberately rejects its matrix, but unconsciously may see itself as cast off and rejected. It considers itself elite and elect. That is, it defends itself against the unconscious view that it is undesirable by putting forward the opposite view. It disputes the religious basis for the authority of the larger society. The larger society claims that its authority derives from divine recognition, while the new fraternity claims that its members experience God directly, hence need not defer to established authority.

From a psychologic point of view, then, certain statements may be made about the mystic:

1. He is an individual who finds living within his society stressful.
2. He retreats from his society and the reality which it sponsors by withdrawing his interest from both and by reinvesting that interest in impressions which arise from within.
3. He takes advantage of his ability to retreat to the

psychic position that existed during his infancy when
the only reality which had access to his consciousness
was the reality of inner sensation.

4. He reinforces his retreat and overcomes the loneliness which it would create by joining with others to
form an elite, democratic, and abstemious mystical
fraternity.

5. He claims authority for his departure from, or rebellion against, the religious establishment by asserting
that he has been granted immediate experience of
the divine which supersedes traditional authority.

9

MYSTICISM AND CREATIVITY

The mystical state resembles not just certain pathological conditions, but also common psychological phenomena that are generally regarded as normal. In romantic love, for example, there is a changed sense of reality in which the overestimation of the loved one approaches the mystic's attitude toward the divine; and in a course that never runs smooth, ecstasy alternates with darkness and suffering. As another example, the esthetic reactions touched off by painting, poetry and music are characterized by a change in the sense of reality in which the external world is significantly distorted or excluded and which is both sublime and ineffable. In still another example, those who are deeply affected by nature see natural objects in terms of human form and feelings, an experience they share with mystics; in fact, identification with nature is so complete for some persons as to be indistinguishable from mystical union.

Feelings of awe experienced toward another human being or nature—like love—can be compared to those phases of mysticism in which there is contact with the divine. Some athletes experience a fusion between their bodies and the environment, and performance may be directly related to success in reaching this state of mind. Like the mystical union, ordinary flashes of insight as well as these other states are experienced passively and spontaneously; none can be elicited by logical thought but they arise from unknown

inner sources through the agency of primary process thinking in which the boundaries between self and object fade or
disappear. Such observations suggest that potential mystics
abound—indeed, that everyone might tap these inner
sources and become a mystic were it not for the inhibitions
and rigidities imposed by early training and the want of
proper motivation. Even so, recent surveys indicate that a
high percentage of the population claims to have had one or
more mystical experiences.

Perhaps the mental phenomenon with the closest
psychological ties to mysticism is creativity, the state in which
the mind integrates a variety of information into a new
configuration. This relationship is recognized not only by
members of modern mystical groups who claim that their
methods will enhance creativity, but by the man who is regarded by many as the foremost creative thinker of our time,
Albert Einstein. He writes, "The most beautiful, the most
profound emotion we can experience is the sensation of the
mystical. It is the fundamental emotion that stands at the
cradle of true art and science."[1] In the last century John
Ruskin conceived of the creative artist as a mystic. The
psychologist Maslow espoused the same idea in a broader
context, relating his "peak experiences" and "B-cognition" to
both mysticism and many varieties of creativity.[2] Kris points
to the origins of the term *inspiration*—the essence of
creativity—in the concept of the creative person as an instrument of the divine; the term itself equates breathing and
spiritual influence.[3]

The idea of the relationship between mysticism and
creativity was recognized in ancient times. Plato's dictum
recognizes the fusion of God and the creative person (em-
bodied in the poet) as well as the state of emptiness that is
prerequisite to achieving the mystic goal. "God," he said,
"takes away the minds of poets . . . in order that we who
hear them may know them to be speaking not of themselves,

who utter these priceless words in a state of unconsciousness, but that God himself is the speaker, and that through them he is conversing with us."

In his monumental study, SCIENCE AND CIVILIZATION IN CHINA, Joseph Needham points to the bond between mysticism and scientific creativity in both the East and the West, at least during certain epochs in world history.[4] This contrasts with the antagonism of rationalists (like Aristotelians, Confucians, and Scholastics) toward scientific progress.

In the West, experimental empiricism—such as displayed by Galileo—found an ally in anti-authoritarian religious mysticism, with "rational" theology lined up against it. The addiction that some seventeenth century biologists had for the Kabbalah hinged on the belief that its mysticism might contribute to their studies. The scientific reforms urged by Francis Bacon, who helped to establish modern science, were, in Needham's view, "put forward as part of a mystical interpretation of the Christian religion." Indeed, Needham concludes, "The association between nature-mysticism and science is to be found embedded in the very foundation of modern (post-Renaissance) scientific thought."

In Islam, too, mystical theology was closely associated with early scientific developments. The same phenomena occurred in China at the time of the ancient philosophical schools. It was the mystical Taoists, rather than the rational, government-sponsored Confucians, who stimulated Chinese scientific discovery. Like mystics in general, the Taoists stressed spontaneity, "inaction," "emptying of the mind," simplicity, tranquility, and "transcendental bliss." Emptying of the mind was intended to rid it of distorting memories, prejudices, and preconceived ideas so that true practical knowledge would flourish. Needham feels that these attitudes resulted in the great inventions of ancient China, such as the use of the water wheel.

The qualities of the mystical mind are not confined to the

artist and the scientist. Some political figures also seem to possess them. Tucker[5] has noted this, and Max Weber has suggested that the political leader is effective not merely because of his position but due to gifts of grace (charisma) "by virtue of which he is set apart from other men and treated as endowed with supernatural, superhuman, or at least specifically exceptional powers or qualities."[6] The ideal charismatic leadership, as originally introduced, was, says Weber, "based upon a transcendent call by a divine being in which both the person called and his followers believe." Like mystics, charismatic leaders tend to appear when large numbers of people are suffering some kind of distress and rationalistic thinkers in positions of power are tied to worn-out, rigid systems.

Einstein has pointed out two motives that lead man to art and science, motives that also lead men to mysticism. The first is negative: "to escape from everyday life with its painful crudity and hopeless dreariness, from the fetters of one's own shifting desires." The second is positive:

> Man tries to make for himself in the fashion that suits him best a simplified and intelligible picture of the world; he then tries to some extent to substitute this cosmos of his for the world of experience, and thus to overcome it. This is what the painter, the poet, the speculative philosopher, and the natural scientist do, each in his own fashion. Each makes this cosmos and its construction the pivot of his emotional life, in order to find in this way peace and security which he cannot find in the narrow whirlpool of personal experience.[7]

When we suggest that the mystic is motivated in his search by disappointment with society, by the need to escape from unacceptable external realities, or by the need to rid himself of depression and the feeling of being a rejected outsider, we are saying much the same that Einstein said about creators. Similarly, when we suggest that in reaching this goal, the mystic at last achieves a sense of belonging and that mystical union symbolizes union with a parental figure from whom he felt estranged, we are only adding details to Einstein's remarks about the positive goals of the creator. Indeed, under different cultural or personal influences the creative person might have become a mystic. While it is true that similar problems face all men, they seem to be especially significant to the mystic and the creator. This may account in some measure for the great amount of energy they both put into their work in their obligatory need to solve these problems.

Three Different Creators

A comparison of three men of enduring fame whose personalities and interests seem remarkably different from each other reveals similarities when looked at from the point of view of mysticism: the irascible painter, Vincent van Gogh, a Dutchman who felt cast out from his church, his country and his family; the profound physicist, Albert Einstein, a sensitive German Jew subjected to the anti-Semitism of his country; and the revered politician, Abraham Lincoln, a poor boy from the American heartland who early learned to live with death and suffering. Each had the mark of the prophet— humility combined with a godlike self-image that contributed to affirmative action rather than mere self-glorification. Each conceived of himself as deeply religious but, like the typical mystic, kept himself apart from the institution and the rituals of the church into which he was born. Each had a personal relationship with his own God, and the desire for union with this God emerged in each of them in his own way.

Vincent van Gogh. In the case of van Gogh, the mystical element emerged only in his work as an artist, following an experience of rebirth. In his earlier role as a student preparing for the ministry and as an evangelist, he showed none of the inspired qualities that emerged later on; indeed, art made their emergence possible. When his works as a whole are studied in connection with his written views of them, it becomes clear that Van Gogh's basic longing and the basic theme of his art is to unite with a divine, heavenly being symbolic of the loving mother for whom he had always longed.[8]

Albert Einstein's discoveries, as he himself assures us, were made possible only by the deep "cosmic feeling" that inspires men and gives them the strength "to remain true to their purpose in spite of countless failures." "In my view," he said, "it is the most important function of art and science to awaken this feeling and keep it alive in those who are receptive to it."[9] Einstein's biographer and colleague, Banesh Hoffman, writes, "Einstein, with his feeling of humility, awe and wonder and his sense of oneness with the universe, belongs with the great religious mystics." Einstein escaped from the painful realities of life to a universe of beauty, perfection, and purity—convinced on a philosophic rather than a scientific basis of "the sublimity and marvelous order which reveal themselves both in nature and the world of thought."[10] Assuming his own ideas to be those of scientists as a group, he wrote:

> Individual existence impresses [the scientist] as a sort of prison and he wants to experience the universe as a single significant whole. . . . His religious feeling takes the form of a rapturous amazement at the harmony of natural law, which reveals an intelligence of such superiority that, compared with it, all the systematic thinking and acting of human beings is an utterly insignificant reflection. This feeling is the guiding principle of his life and work, insofar as he succeeds in keeping himself from the shackles of selfish desire. It is beyond question closely akin to that which has possessed the religious geniuses of all ages.[11]

Perhaps through his deep instinctive belief in cosmic unity he strove to discover a unified field theory and to merge space and time into a nondifferentiated unity.

Abraham Lincoln. It has been pointed out that the aspect of Lincoln as a religious mystic has been largely ignored. Just as art became the vehicle for van Gogh's expression and physics became Einstein's vehicle for expressing it, Lincoln's mysticism seems to have emerged with his coming to the presidency, an act that he also experienced as a rebirth. Lincoln's obsession to save the Union (which from a genetic point of view may have been a continuation of his youthful success in preserving the marriage union of his friends the _____s) seems to have been propelled by an inspired faith in God, "trusting in Him who can go with me and remain with you." Solomon Schechter, speaking of Lincoln's aims as President, said, "The *dynamis* of an idea or ideas was indispensable. And this idea defined by the word 'union' was a mystical one as every religious idea is."[12] The Confederate historian, Alexander H. Stephens, commented on Lincoln in a similar vein: "The Union with him in sentiment rose to the sublimity of a religious mysticism."[13]

*   *   *   *

While these examples do not show that creative people, including charismatic political leaders, are all mystics at heart, they do suggest that further study of them from this point of view might prove fruitful. Even without such study, however, we can point to similarities between many creative men and the mystic in terms of their actions and beliefs, the motivations that set them into being, and their psychodynamics. Both the creator and the mystic appear to have anti-establishment tendencies; they defy authority and often find themselves in confrontation with church, government, community or the Academy. Both aim to create a new world image—whether in a spiritual or an ideological sense, in words, on canvas, in music, in mathematics, in the laboratory, or in political action. They often experience this new image as a phenomenon of rebirth or speak of the "pangs of birth." Their goal is to create new solutions to old problems and in doing so change their view of themselves and of the world as well. For the most part, they wish to create a revolution in men's minds, but when pushed to it may become militant in the service of their cause. Those who are more passive or who feel more threatened by personal encounter may furnish the ideas for new movements, while more active physical types furnish the brawn. Whatever their contribution, both are often regarded with a mixture of suspicion and awe by the community.

Like the mystic, the creator is imbued with intense desire and boundless energy. As the mystic seeks the joyous moment of union, the creator seeks the thrill of the creative moment. Even if fame and fortune are thrust upon him, he tends to live a humble or even an ascetic life. He does not appear to be self-seeking, although at an unconscious level he often identifies himself with grandiose figures.

Syncretism, a type of thinking that unites or reconciles diverse ideas, seems to be an important facet of the thinking of both mystics and creators, one that is essential to their aims. Perhaps related to it, the synesthesia noted in mystics is also seen in artists, as witness their not uncommon references to a mutual relationship between colors and musical tones. Like mystics, creators frequently project their inner fantasies, self-image, and emotions into the external world, attributing personal meaning to objects and to other individuals. This is exemplified by the artist's perception of the tree in terms of human thoughts and feelings. The tendency, however, is no doubt common among many highly creative people, regardless of their field of endeavor. In the words of one young woman undergoing psychoanalysis,

> When I look at leaves in the tree outside the window there is a continuity between me and them except for a thinning out in be-

tween. When you drink water, you are drinking dinosaur's piss. You are electrified by touching grass, because grass is the hair of the ground. And you'd better tread lightly or you'll injure the ground's brain. You hug a tree and you cut and scratch your hands doing it and you like it—like childbirth, it's something valuable. You're destroying yourself yes, but you're born again. That's God. Do you disappear with the climax? Yes, but you're reborn when you fight and kiss and make up. You get killed so you can be reborn.

This explanation illustrates the way the external world is perceived by the creator as well as the mystic. When deeply involved in their work, both are able to distort the external world in terms of inner perceptions, or exclude it altogether. At the same time, intense or external perceptions may be heightened, and this sensitivity may open the path to hidden aspects of reality.

Like the mystic, the creator seeks solitude. Indeed, the ability to tolerate solitude is required by the goals of both, for only in solitude can the mind work out the new mental configuration it seeks. While this ability may be autonomous, it may have developed out of a fear of intimacy and the need to handle the loneliness that accompanies isolation. Some creative people find that the solitary quest for new ideas alleviates their loneliness, and this quest then becomes a powerful force that stimulates creative thinking.

Like the mystic, the creator often does not isolate himself totally from human contact, but tends to form small, close-knit groups with others having common interests and goals. These groups may not only provide a source of new ideas but also help to contain loneliness while avoiding the feared or hated authoritarians of the Establishment. Furthermore, the democratic nature of the group discourages the development of new authoritarians and helps to maintain self-esteem.

The mystic's love of the Divine and his desire to be intimate with Him has its counterpart in the creator's devotion to nature and natural laws and his desire to understand them as no one has ever understood them before—whether this be in artistic, scientific or philosophic terms. This relationship, like the mystic's with Divinity, is personal and direct. In contrast, the hack artist or routine scientist uses others much as the ordinary churchgoer uses the priest. Both the mystic and the creator commonly find a haven in the use of symbols: the artist, for example, in the color, form or object to which he attaches special significance; the scientist in mathematics (a subject also dear to the hearts of many mystics), or in an esoteric vocabulary known only to initiates.

The alternating moods of depression and joy characteristic of the Mystic Way find their counterpart in the powerful mood swings of many creators, forming a common enough pattern to warrant suggesting a "creative-depressive person-ality" comparable to that of the manic-depressive.[14] (The creative phase, like the manic phase, is marked by a tre-mendous output of energy but differs from the latter in having clear-cut goals.) The mystic's "illumination" is analogous to the "inspiration" of the creator. In both, the periods in which old information is brought together in new and exciting patterns seem to appear spontaneously and passively, as if on a blank screen. Inspiration is a time when previous ideas and observations fit together like the pieces of a puzzle, doubts and depression disappear and the certainty of "ultimate truth" takes their place.

Before the mystic can be illuminated or the creator in-spired, there is a long period during which each of them actively acquires and stores information. The mystic acquires a knowledge of religions and philosophy, the artist a knowl-edge of art styles and techniques, the scientist a knowledge of prior work in related fields, and the creative political leader a knowledge of history. Characteristically, however, neither the mystic nor the creator is bound to his predecessors; he makes use of whatever is compatible with his own needs and discards the rest. Once having accumulated enough information for their needs, the mystic and the creator are able to forego active, logical, goal-seeking behavior. They "empty the mind" and enter a seemingly passive state in which the preconscious, cooperating with the unconscious, selectively integrates and rejects information before spontaneously coming up with a solution. This alternation between prelogical and logical mental processes—that is, between primary process and secondary process thinking—may be carried out repeatedly before the solution is finally achieved. Claude Bernard, the father of experimental medicine, has pointed out the danger of excessive trust in pure logic and the necessity for alternating between free use of the imagination and reason in controlled experimentation. He cites the need to be "ignorant," that is, to empty the mind, for he believed that experimental ideas are based on intuitions which appear "with the rapidity of lightning, and as a sudden revelation." [15] These subjective truths, he adds, are experienced as absolute, reminiscent of the mystic. Similar things might be said about creative thinking in other fields.

Linear, logical thought is not, then, the essential core of creativity but an essential means of assessing, controlling, modifying and synthesizing created elements into a meaningful whole. Primary process creates indiscriminately, as it were; secondary process evaluates what is created. Arieti has called this ongoing interplay "tertiary process," [16] ascribing to this fusion of primary and secondary processes emergent qualities not implicit in either component taken alone. The psychologist Guilford [17] has approached intellect from the point of view of multivariate factor analysis and concludes that there is no one problem-solving (creative) ability—rather there are cognitive operations (understanding the problem), productive operations (generating steps toward a solution), evaluative operations (of understanding and production), and generally distinct memory operations as well. Thus the methodologically more sophisticated factor-analytic approach yields a conclusion not very different from the incomparably richer clinical psychoanalytic approach.

References

1. Albert Einstein. IDEAS AND OPINIONS (New York: Crown Publishers, 1954).
2. Abraham H. Maslow. TOWARD A PSYCHOLOGY OF BEING, 2nd ed. (New York: D. Van Nostrand, 1968) paperback.
3. Ernst Kris. PSYCHOANALYTIC EXPLORATIONS IN ART (New York: International Universities Press, 1952) p 291.
4. Joseph Needham. SCIENCE AND CIVILIZATION IN CHINA, Vol. 2 of HISTORY OF SCIENTIFIC THOUGHT (Cambridge: University Press, 1956).
5. Robert C. Tucker. The Theory of Charismatic Leadership. *Daedalus* (Summer 1968) pp 731–756.
6. Max Weber. THEORY OF SOCIAL AND ECONOMIC ORGANIZATION (New York: Oxford University Press, 1947).
7. See reference 1 above, p 75.
8. Albert J. Lubin. STRANGER ON THE EARTH: A PSYCHOLOGICAL BIOGRAPHY OF VINCENT VAN GOGH (New York: Holt, Rinehart & Winston, 1972).
9. See reference 1 above, p 75.
10. Banesh Hoffman. ALBERT EINSTEIN (New York: Viking Press, 1972).
11. See reference 1 above, p 75.
12. Solomon Schechter. ABRAHAM LINCOLN: A TRIBUTE OF THE SYNAGOGUE, Emanuel Hertz, Ed. (New York: Bloch Publishing, 1927) pp 383–400.
13. Alexander H. Stephens in PATRIOTIC GORE: STUDIES IN THE LITERATURE OF THE AMERICAN CIVIL WAR, Edmund Wilson, Ed. (New York: Oxford University Press, 1962).
14. Albert J. Lubin. "From Augustine to Einstein: Some Thoughts on Mysticism, Creativity, and Identity." Paper presented at the San Francisco Psychoanalytic Institute, January 6, 1975.
15. Claude Bernard. AN INTRODUCTION TO THE STUDY OF EXPERIMENTAL MEDICINE (New York: Macmillan, 1927).
16. Silvano Arieti. AMERICAN HANDBOOK OF PSYCHIATRY, Vol. II (New York: Basic Books, 1959).
17. J. P. Guilford. THE NATURE OF HUMAN INTELLIGENCE (New York: McGraw Hill, 1967).

10

CASE REPORT: A MYSTICAL EXPERIENCE

Mystical experiences are rarely observed in psychotherapeutic practice. As Sterba has noted, mystics tend to be healers rather than patients.[1] One such experience has come to our attention, however, wherein the patient was also a healer. A description of this experience and of the circumstances leading up to it may help to illustrate some of the psychological phenomena that have been discussed in the two previous chapters.

The patient, a woman in her early thirties, was reared by a fanatically religious, highly neurotic mother who was a convert to the Seventh-Day Adventist Church. During the child's rearing, the mother had described direct, unmediated experiences with God. The daughter was an active participant in the church and followed its prohibitions against such sins as dancing, movie-going, and the use of make-up. During an argument with her mother when she was 15 years old, she turned against the Church, cursing her parents, Christ, and God.

At the age of 19 she began a life of promiscuity and wandering, not unlike that of Saint Augustine at the same stage of life. Male sex partners were marked by low status and lack of character, contrasting with the status and character of her successful father. She obtained little gratification from these sexual experiences and suffered more guilt about them than she was willing to admit to herself at the time. She

came for treatment because of frequent spells of hopeless-
ness and depression associated with the conviction that she
would eventually commit suicide. Her life had always been
chaotic, whether at home or in her travels, and she sought
the certainty that would come with self-knowledge, harbor-
ing a strong faith that self-knowledge guarantees cure.

On the positive side, she had an engaging personality,
somewhat theatrical and often funny, that attracted many
people. A more substantial asset, however, was her talent as
an intuitive psychotherapist who used art as her chief
technique in treating small groups. Her success in this field
was linked with a belief that she had an uncanny ability to
understand deeper motivations, a belief that was not without
foundation, for, like Saint Augustine, she was a good
psychologist.

The original target for her therapeutic skills was her parents. The mother had spent much of her life in intimate
professional liaisons with internists, psychiatrists and sur-
geons due to a host of psychosomatic disorders; she dominated her husband, who quietly went along with her excesses. The girl was forever frustrated in her therapeutic attempts with them and forever angry because they refused to
see the light and change their ways. She had two brothers,
one older, one younger, who were constantly battling with
their parents. From an early age, she felt obliged to bring the
family together, a task for Sisyphus. The younger brother,
she felt, was neglected by a sick mother, and the girl assumed
the mother's place with him. About a year before she came
for therapy, he became psychotic. This made her feel she
had failed in her task, and she blamed herself for his illness.

On entering therapy she found it impossible to lie on the
couch. After some delay, she reluctantly admitted being ter-
rified that the therapist would lose control and attempt some
strange and perverse sexual act with her, a deed that would
bring an end to the treatment and destroy her hope for a

cure. At the same time she did not feel the slightest sexual attraction to the therapist. After all, he was old enough to be her father and, she reiterated, her father had never been sexually attractive to her. It also became clear, however, that fear of being controlled by the therapist made it imperative for her to control the therapeutic situation, and she felt able to do this only while facing him.

During the two years that followed, she continued to face the therapist, keeping track of his every move and expression. Her fear diminished without entirely disappearing, and she no longer felt impelled to carry on sexual exploits with delinquent men. While on a brief outing, she had a dream she regarded as highly significant. Yet for two weeks she deliberately withheld mention of it. Disturbed by her need to control the therapeutic relationship, she decided to lie on the couch once again and give up control. Once on it, she related the dream.

The account of the dream should be prefaced. One year before, almost to the day, she announced to the therapist that she had become a new woman and would no longer be controlling. Both the announcement and her return to the couch followed shortly after the therapist's notice to her of his forthcoming vacation. Becoming a new, noncontrolling person "proved" she was cured—it was a way of reassuring herself that she could get along without him. But behind her controls were powerful longings to be dependent on him. This mirrored her childhood situation: Because her parents were unable to gratify her dependency needs, she reacted by trying to control them in her role as family therapist.

Now to return to the dream. She beheld an enormous spider covered with a protective shell. Its hairy legs resembled the bars of a jail, and her father was confined inside them. The leg-bars, however, were far enough apart for him to escape, but he stupidly chose to remain. She assumed that the spider represented her mother (spider-mothers had been

the subject of previous discussions concerning a severe
spider phobia and the fact that spiders or insects entered into
her dreams). The shell encasing the spider in this latest
dream prevented her from crushing the creature, an idea
that reflected the fear of her murderous rage toward her
mother.

Fascinated by the dream, she discussed it with some
friends after the therapy session. One of them, a man, volun-
teered that the shell also prevented her from killing her
father, for if the spider-mother was crushed, the father
would also be crushed. This idea, while potentially distressing, was an exciting eye-opener. At her suggestion, she
accompanied the fellow to his apartment to continue the
discussion, incidentally wondering whether he might be in-
terested in her as a woman, even though she was not in-
terested in him as a man. Soon, however, this idea was laid to
rest by the appearance of his girlfriend, but she felt no
disappointment. Indeed, she became increasingly exuberant.

Returning home, she found her mind working at great
speed, like a computerized loom, weaving together in a marvelous pattern the varied loose strands of her life which at
the same time revealed a new and exciting view of the universe with which she felt at one. She felt that she was acquiring great knowledge, that everything was comprehensible
and beautiful, and she found herself in a state of ecstasy. For
a moment she feared she might be losing her mind. This led
to a fantasy in which the therapist came to her aid but she
stabbed him as he entered the room. Only later did she relate
this fantasied act to the earlier idea of killing her father.

During this revelation, she looked into the depths of her
soul, where it was so clear that it went on forever. Then she
looked outward, and there too it was so clear that she could
look into infinity. A cosmic eye appeared before her, her own
projected self-observation. At first, its expression was
malevolent, but suddenly it winked, and she laughed. "Of

course," she thought, "the answer I've been searching is within me and all around me. It's been there all the time." From seeing the totality of herself and the universe, she knew where she came from and where she fit in, acknowledging that she was part of a giant historical process. She experienced God—not *a* god but something that projected her into a higher state of being (which she later called "cosmic consciousness") and that was indescribable. Hazy golden figures of superior intelligence, not of this earth, appeared in a light and ethereal atmosphere (probably reminiscent of the heaven of her childhood). The scene seemed real at the time but later on she recognized it as symbolic.

She also perceived in her mind's eye a tall vertical structure resembling a rocket. It was charged with good and evil energy; the tension between the two created a pressure in its center that propelled it forward. Knowledge arising under it added to its force. It was about to explode into space, like a penis on the point of orgasm, and she regarded it as a sign of conception and rebirth. The rocket-penis then changed into a connected series of penises and vaginas that formed the symbol for infinity. This structure was at the center of the universe. She wondered whether the universe was in a stagnating state of balance between good and evil or was slowly advancing as the result of self-knowledge and communication. She decided that it was advancing.

These visions represented for her the unity of the human condition and the universe, the same energy ordering both. She concluded that an understanding of the universe can only be gained by understanding oneself. The vertically directed structure was also reminiscent of a childhood dream in which she floated (was "translated") up into heaven, where Christ awaited her; and a more recent dream of flying into the sky.

She talked freely about the experience, but questions brought only vague answers. She remarked, as so many mystics have remarked, that it was impossible to describe clearly. Her mood was ecstatic (if you prefer a theological term) or euphoric (if you prefer psychiatric vocabulary); it persisted for about ten days. She felt that everything in her life had led up to this momentous experience and that all of her knowledge had become reorganized during its course. For her, the most important gain from it was a conviction that she was a worthwhile person with worthwhile ideas, not the intrinsically evil person, "rotten to the core," that her mother had convinced her she was. Therefore, she was no longer suspicious of others and no longer feared lying on the couch.

Conditioned by her state of ecstasy, she was convinced that her problems were basically solved, even though she would have occasional unhappy periods in her life. She felt no need for further treatment, but would continue her sessions in order to help the therapist understand her experience, for which she gave him credit. With a certain tongue-in-cheek reticence, she said she may have been chosen for it in order to help the world. From family healer, to group therapist, to world savior!

Because understanding herself and understanding the universe were interdependent, she developed new intellectual interests. She began to study and discuss astronomy, anthropology and philosophy, overcoming a lifelong inhibition to reading serious literature.

During the sessions that followed, she expressed anger toward her father for refusing to extricate himself from his neurotic wife's trap, interpreting this as a rejection of herself. It was clear that rejection by a man is an important theme in her life. Early in puberty, she had developed a strong sexual attraction to her older brother, who had been sexually active from an early age. He rejected her for a sexual relationship with her closest girlfriend. Later she attached these feelings to numerous nameless men. And the therapist's approaching vacation would be another rejection. Perhaps the event at her friend's apartment that preceded her mystical experience, when the thought that the fellow might care for her was destroyed by his girlfriend's appearance, was still another rejection.

Soon after the experience she visited her parents, where she became aware of an idea that must have been inside her "forever." When her father made awkward attempts to touch or hold her, she feared—as she feared in her treatment sessions with the therapist—that his mind would crack and he would attempt some horrible, degrading sexual act with her. This recalled an incident when she was 18, the year before she began her life of promiscuity. Left alone at night during her mother's absence, she slept in her parents' bed, knowing her father would return later. She then had a horrifying fantasy that on his return her presence there would cause him to lose control over his sexual desires, and she, furiously indignant, would ruin him. She herself concluded that her fantasy about the therapist was "transferred" from these earlier fantasies about her father. But when the therapist suggested that her fear was originally derived from her own unconscious sexual attachment to the father, and that her sexual attraction toward her brother during puberty was a continuation of this earlier attachment, she disagreed.

Among other insights that she acquired during the ecstatic phase of her experience and the days that followed, she recognized that fear of her own murderous rage had made it difficult to listen to others about herself and important for her always to be right, "or else," she said, "I'd know my own evil." Now this rage no longer felt so dangerous. She also recognized that her mystical experience helped to alleviate her distress about her brother's psychosis and her guilt about it, for some of the revelations in her experience were similar to her brother's ideas, which she now understood. As a result, while continuing to accept his illness, she could believe that some of his ideas about God were correct: he had some keen insights and might yet accomplish something.

It took her longer, however, to see another side to the

dream, to see that she herself was the controlling spider, and the father beneath her also represented the therapist. He was kept in place, unable to leave her. The vertical structure that resembled a penis on the point of orgasm and subsequent ideas about "cloning" (the ability to reproduce without benefit of a partner, similar to the Immaculate Conception by the Virgin Mary) led the therapist to suggest that the father between her legs might also represent her own penis, enabling her to be a self-contained entity without need of a man. She could not agree with this suggestion but it reminded her that unlike her real father, her dream father had an absolutely bald head. It also reminded her that her mother had pictured her father to her as a big penis and that only the mother's control prevented him from being a sexual maniac. She also believed that her experience, dealing as it did with rebirth and immortality, helped her to handle her fears of death.

The ecstasy and the curious ideation of the mystical experience might suggest a manic or schizophrenic state. In contrast to what is usually seen in such conditions, however, her personal relationships and her therapeutic skills appeared unimpaired; her appraisal of real-life situations as well as her insight into herself seemed more rather than less acute; her concentration was improved; and her goals seemed more certain. The experience seemed to be more integrating than disintegrating. One might also perceive it as a dramatic hysterical attack, and this would also be difficult to disprove.

So, while a psychiatric diagnosis cannot be dismissed, her experience was certainly akin to those described by great religious mystics who have found a new life through them.

The psychological phenomena seen in this patient resemble those we have described in well-known mystics. The mystical experience appeared against a background of mental anguish. It consisted of a withdrawal of interest from the real world and its problems, the acknowledgment of which would have released feelings of abandonment and depression. Her interests were reinvested in a fantasy universe, representing God, in which such problems do not exist, and she felt herself united with this God-universe, a substitute for an unavailable or rejecting parent. The mystical union made up for the rejection she feared from her father, now represented by the therapist and another man.

The search for knowledge that often precedes mystical states was sought in a psychotherapeutic experience. The mystical state itself provided the illusion of knowledge. But unlike many mystical states, in which the search ends with the illusion, it stimulated her to seek further knowledge and led directly to the disappearance of her inhibition to serious reading. This continued search is characteristic of those in whom mystical states contribute toward creative activity. What the future holds for her, of course, remains to be seen, yet the event seems able to stand on its own, with the reasonable possibility that it will eventually prove to be beneficial for herself and, since she is a creative and therapeutic person, for society.

Reference

1. Richard Sterba. Remarks on Mystic States. *American Imago* 25 (1968):77–85.

11

CONCLUSION

The occasional solitary mystic (as distinguished from the member of a mystical movement) exhibits behavior or describes experiences which are often held unacceptable to the society in which he lives. Such individuals are considered aberrant in terms of some criteria significant within that society—for example, they may be labeled crazy, immoral, possessed, blasphemous, unconventional or irresponsible, and frequently they elicit hostility and condemnation. As psychiatrists, reading the recorded descriptions of mystical states, we might well be inclined to make a diagnosis of some serious mental illness, most frequently hysteria or schizophrenia; occasionally, manic-depressive illness.

Whatever form the mystical behavior takes, it implies repudiation of some important aspect of society—its conduct, its standards, or its expectations. The interest of this Committee in writing this report derives from the fact that mysticism has become a significant social force in our time, and we should like to make a start at a psychological approach to it. The mystic has been observed in many instances as able and, in fact, eager to enter into social relations with other individuals. Therefore, given a situation of severe internal stress or a general cultural crisis as now exists, many such persons may resort to mystical practice, then agglomerate with others to form a mystical group, and, under the influence of a suitable leader, found a movement.

At their inception, mystical movements seem always to challenge an existing social order. It is typical of their history that at the outset they undertake to denounce misbehavior of the society in which they live. Every mystical movement attempts to reform the society or to rebel against it. The degree of rebellion and its nature may vary. For example, members of one movement may merely secede from the larger society, labeling it as evil, like the Dead Sea Sects and the Essenes; those of another may encourage a change in popular standards and practices, as did the Hassidim; others may threaten the institutions of the society, religious or political, as did the Quakers.

In some instances the leader of such a mystical movement is designated as a messiah. The word means "anointed" and therefore implies that the messiah is the supreme authority, having been called by God himself. A group with a messianic leader tends to move toward active political or social revolt. The biblical prophets, on the other hand, some of whom were mystical but none of them messianic, encouraged social and religious reform. Groups which are waiting for the advent of a messiah may encourage either secession from society or merely a quietistic acceptance.

The fate of a mystical movement depends on the readiness of the population to support it, the ability and sanity of its leader, and the strength of the established institutions which it challenges. For example, a mystical movement may quietly die, and probably most do; it may undertake revolutionary activity and be defeated, as were the followers of Bar Kochba, who led a Judean revolt against Rome in the year 135 of this era; it may be accepted as a subordinate organization within the establishment and used by the latter against its own enemies, as were the Jesuits. Often enough in the history of mystical movements, we find that the movement starts as a rebellion against an established authority and may subsequently replace it. With the weakening of its revolutionary ardor and purity it lapses into the same weaknesses and faults as its predecessor, invoking a similar challenge from a successor. This sequence is not especially characteristic of religious or mystical movements, but rather of successful revolutionary movements, whatever their nature.

As noted, some observers believe that some mystical movements have appeared in response to external stress. For example, the Dead Sea Sects arose in a population torn by factional conflict generated by the attraction to Hellenism on the one hand and loyalty to Jewish purity on the other. Lurianic mysticism of sixteenth century Safed and its derivative Sabbataian movement of the seventeenth century in Eastern Europe are movements usually attributed to the expulsion and destruction of the powerful Jewish community of Spain at the end of the fifteenth century. Nationalism and culture clash can be adduced to account for the rise of mystical movements in modern India. The Quakers appeared in the midst of the English civil war.

There are other mystical movements, however, in which these stressful pressures cannot easily be discerned. For example, Kabbalistic mysticism of the *Zohar* appeared in the Jewish community of Spain at the end of the thirteenth century, when that community was vigorous, prosperous, respected and flourishing.

In our own culture, mystical movements nowadays attract especially the young people (although we do not know to what extent this has always been true), and it is this same youthful population which provides the members of other dissident movements. Therefore, we should seriously consider the possibility that some change has occurred in our society—not as a result of external pressure but as a result of inner disequilibrium—which places adolescents and young adults under special stress. If that is so, then their attacks on society would be correctly addressed, although the message may be incorrect. As psychiatrists, we know that the transition of the young person from adolescent to adult is an ordeal. Many make this transition easily and gracefully and conventionally; a few never make it and become mentally ill; a large minority make it through some spiritual discipline or through social and political action.

In attempting to account for the current disposition of young people to turn to mysticism, some but not all participants in this study were impressed by the interaction between external social stress and psychic disorder. According to their view, a society which places obstacles in the way of the young person's transition to adulthood is imposing an additional stress on him. The relative comfort and prosperity of our society suggest the possibility that the absence of any challenge constitutes just such a stress. If it does, this would imply that challenge facilitates maturation and its absence retards the process. Actually, the process of maturation in adolescence requires a moderate degree of challenge. Challenge of a degree lesser or greater than the optimal constitutes a stress which may retard the process. The healthy adolescent may well be able to advance despite that stress. However, the marginal adolescent will succumb, lapsing into illness or turning to one of the acting-out defenses against illness.

To place this view in context, the current disposition of some young people to turn to mysticism represents an effort by various groupings of them in a state of marginal mental health to defend against the stresses of a society which has disappointed them by offering them insufficient external challenge. Of those who choose the mystical way of life, it is hard to say which ones are moving toward conflict resolution and which toward psychic breakdown. In any case they are all to some extent engaged in an attack on their parents' standards as representative of the established social order.

Side by side with this struggle with values of family and society is a tendency to turn aside from the difficult problems

of the mundane by what amounts to a flight through introversion. Political and social ambiguities which present insu-
perable difficulties of solution are ignored in favor of a private
salvation and world view. Further, personal conflicts and
existential cravings are at least temporarily denied, replaced
by ecstatic or meditational practices. These resolutions may
or may not be stable.

Additional factors characteristic of our own day and culture are believed by some to encourage mystical practice.
One such factor often cited is the feeling of discouragement
and powerlessness in the face of threatened nuclear
holocaust. Second is the generalized breakdown of social and
ethical norms of traditional Western culture. Third is the
decline in authority of heretofore accepted religious teachings. Fourth, comfort itself may cease to be desirable and
favor a turning to nonmaterial satisfactions. Finally, the positive intellectual and material success of modern science may
have led many persons to seek experiences that transcend
the wholly rational. In this connection, modern physical scientists, in their search for fundamental unifying concepts,
seem at times to be on their own mystical quest.

Since these factors are operative for all, it is to be understood that neurotic and psychotic sufferers will be especially
tempted to seek relief of pain through transcendent experience. These attempted integrations can fail or, if built on too
much internal disturbance, can be destructive by furthering
delusions or increasing maladaptation.

There has been much debate over the use of psychedelic
drugs to provide "instant" mystical experience. It is clear that
these drugs can indeed be used to achieve transcendent and
ecstatic states. However, it is unclear how much long-term
value can be gained from the drug experience even when the
subject has also undergone prior training and mental discipline in order to integrate it.

The ambiguity of the mystical personality, in history and

on the current scene, is perhaps illustrated by the fact that no single generalization can be made to account for it. Historical studies or clinical observations of many mystics point primarily toward antisocial and pathological variables; studies of other mystics lead to an appreciation of their contributions and creativity; observations of still others show that the two attributes apparently can and do coexist in the same personality.

It will be of interest to see how the current prevalence of mysticism will be affected by changes in those conditions which are usually assumed to be congenial to it.

EPILOGUE

A subject that brings together the largest audience ever to attend a meeting of the American Psychiatric Association and that causes a world potentate, the Shah of Iran, to assert that "mystical intuition" prevents him from making mistakes deserves more than we have been able to give it. Because of this, we feel tempted to transcend our knowledge in this epilogue.

When put to it, however, we find it difficult to add significantly to our conclusions regarding the relations between society and the individual, and how they have contributed to the rise of mysticism, as well as the relationship between mystical movements of the past and the current mystical scene. In consequence, we shall reserve our final remarks for other subjects.

The inability of this Committee to make a firm distinction between a mystical state and a psychopathological state may be due, in part at least, to more fundamental theoretical problems in psychiatry. The many ways in which human behavior and thought can be perceived make numerous points of view inevitable. For example, there are those who draw fine lines between various psychiatric disorders and, on the other hand, those who regard all psychiatric diagnoses as irrelevant and who perceive in schizophrenia a manifestation to be prized as a way toward better adaptation. Pathology may be uncovered in the nature of—and the method of resolution of—the conflicts in someone who seems to be brimming over with mental health, while the thought and behavior of the most disturbed patient may be viewed as a contribution to his well-being. Therefore we should not expect to be able to reach a consensus on the line distinguishing mysticism from mental disorder. From one point of view all mystical experiences may be regarded as symptoms of mental disturbance, and from another, they may be regarded as attempts at adaptation.

By and large, the psychoanalytic orientation of the majority of the Committee on Psychiatry and Religion has determined the approach to this report. Given that psychoanalysis is an open-ended theoretical system, we might have gone further with our psychoanalytic interpretation had caution or disagreement not stopped us. For one thing, we might have expanded our discussion on the nature of the childhood events that contribute to adult proclivities toward mysticism. To cite one example, we could have theorized about a possible connection between the development of awe in childhood and mystical states in adulthood. Saint Catherine of Siena was a mystic who reported having highly developed feelings of awe at the age of five, when she saw the Lord "in the most sacred and awe-inspiring garb imaginable" above the Sienese church of San Domenico. Greenacre has suggested that childhood feelings of awe which may later be associated with inspiration, creativity and religious feeling are often derived from awe (as distinguished from envy) of the phallus.[1,2] In the girl, awe is more liable to be aroused, according to Greenacre, if the child sees an adult phallus rather than a boy's.

Other psychoanalytic hypotheses regarding the psychology of mysticism were proposed, but the Committee as a whole decided to exclude them from the body of this report. For one, Horton has suggested that the mystical experience is an adult version of the "transitional phenomenon" described by Winnicot—"an intermediate area of experience . . . symbolical of some past object, such as the breast . . . a neutral area of experience which will not be challenged." An example is a fetish object, such as a special blanket or doll, that the child clutches and cherishes.[3] Winnicott described it as the "substance of an *illusion*, that which is allowed to the infant, and which in adult life is inherent in art and religion."[4] Horton points out several similarities: (1) Both experiences entail a blending of perceived inner and outer psychic reality; (2) both experiences have soothing functions and may be derived from the child's internalization of the mothering figure; (3) neither experience is challengeable; (4) both experiences come to be more important than the mother, an "almost inseparable part"; and (5) both exhibit maturational potential, providing a needed impetus for separation and individuation. Like the transitional phenomenon, the mystical experience may become an adaptive ego mechanism of defense.

Oremland, using Winnicott's idea, comes up with a different interpretation. He theorizes that creative states and mystical states can be differentiated: Creativity is "part of the transitional process with its emerging sense of separateness and individuation . . . a movement from the monadic to the dyadic," a reexperiencing of the first "not me" world. In contrast, the mystical state differs from transitional phenomena in that it moves from the dyadic system to the monadic system, to a fusion between inside and outside; hence, it evolves from phenomena that occur developmentally earlier than transitional phenomena. Because of this, the need for communication is eliminated, and in this respect as well, mysticism differs from creativity.[5]

Deikman makes use of the concepts of automatization of Hartmann and of deautomatization of Gill and Brenman in explaining the dynamics of mystical states. Automatization permits us to carry on our usual activities without having to figure out each complicated step. Deautomization signifies a breakdown in this process. Deikman has suggested that deautomatization takes place in the mystic; and because stimulus-processing is less efficient in deautomatization, the mystic is enabled to discover new or long-forgotten experiences, as well as cognitive or sensory states that had been excluded by the rigidities of automatization. This same process may apply equally to creativity.[6,7]

In writing about creative thinking in THE HIDDEN ORDER OF ART, Anton Ehrenzweig has proposed a different concept, using "dedifferentiation" as his key term. Differentiation refers to the gradually increasing ability to make distinctions, beginning with the distinction between self and object; dedifferentiation signifies the loss or suspension of this ability. Acknowledging the similarity between mysticism and creativity, Ehrenzweig writes, "Any—not only religious—creative experience can produce an oceanic state. In my view this state need not to be due to a 'regression' to an infantile state, but could be the product of extreme dedifferentiation in lower levels of the ego which occurs during creative work. Dedifferentiation suspends many kinds of boundaries and distinctions, . . . [inducing] a mystic oceanic feeling that is distinctively manic in character [using *manic* in the Kleinian sense]. . . . Dedifferentiation transforms reality according to the structural principles valid on those deeper levels." In the process, Ehrenzweig notes, "perfect integration is possible because of unlimited mutual interpenetration of oceanic imagery."[8]

The stress on absence of automatization, on loss of efficiency in stimulus-processing, and on the absence of differentiation seems to obscure the extraordinary complexity of the events that take place in the psyche, and the speed at which they occur, so bewildering that the sluggish conscious mind cannot keep up with them any more than a mathematician can keep up with a computer. Highly creative people and high-level mystics are able to function in hyperautomatized ways, capable of finer differentiations than others, even though they may have gone through a chaotic, seemingly undifferentiated experience before they

got there. It is the final differentiation, bringing supreme
order out of chaos, that is significant, not the fact of chaos—a
state that most of us, at least those who are not terribly rigid,
have no difficulty at all in experiencing.

Looking at mysticism from the point of view of identity
formation, it can be seen as a different though parallel process.[9] Identity is a unique integration of psychological, social,
historical and educational attributes which, when successful,
results in a harmonious human being. In this view, mystical
experiences, like creative experiences, are attempts at integration or reintegration by people who have not achieved
satisfying results in identity formation or, to put it another
way, have too many conflicts that cannot be resolved har-
moniously. Identity formation is associated with internal resolution and is more or less permanent. In creativity, the
resolution is projecting outside of the mind (as in a painting
or a scientific discovery) and in itself does not involve a
permanent change in the creator. Hence, it needs to be
repeated again and again. Perhaps from this point of view
mystical processes lie between identity formation and creativity, because the integrative process, involving the projection
of images of the self and of others into theological or natural
forces, may, if successful, initiate permanent changes in the
personality or identity.

In the analytic psychology of Jung, himself a mystic, mysticism is held to be a fundamental category of human experience. Eric Neumann, in particular, has discussed mysticism
from a Jungian point of view. Man, he writes, is a *Homo
mysticus*. Mystical phenomena contribute to personality development and are essential to all creative processes. Mystical
experiences are not only theistic, but atheistic, pantheistic,
materialistic, idealistic, extroverted and introverted. They
give rise to love, artistic creation, great ideas and delusions.
While Neumann agrees with Freudian psychoanalysts that
projection plays a role in mysticism, he believes that the

failure of many analysts to recognize the vital significance of archetypes and the collective unconscious gives rise to psychoanalytic interpretations that are reductionistic and personalistic. For mysticism is grounded in the encounter between the ego and the numinous (the supernatural presence, as perceived) that takes place deep in the collective unconscious. Because of this, mysticism is inherent in man, and every mystical experience (or, in Jungian terms, every encounter between the ego and the numinous) transforms his personality, and what is more, "the development of [man's] natural phases with their archetypal encounters gives a mystical stamp to the development of every man, even though he may be unaware of it."[10]

Of especial interest to students of mysticism is Neumann's statement that mysticism originates in childhood and continues to metamorphose throughout life. Man is "in constant mystical motion." The many varieties of mysticism appear in relation to developmental phases in the individual. Among them, several stand out as contrasting forms.

Source mysticism, or "uroborus mysticism," is seen in children, in primitive people, and in pathological and unstable personalities. It appears when man cannot face conflict but yearns to return to the paradise of the maternal womb or the Great Mother archetype, a state known as "uroborus incest." Nihilistic, its aim is world-destructive, and it is noncreative.

Hero mysticism, or "the Fight with the Dragon," is characteristic of puberty and early adulthood. In it, conflict and life in this world are accepted; its mission is world-transforming. Instead of a return to the Great Mother-Womb, there is union with the Godhead or one of the great archetypal leaders. The story of David and Goliath exemplifies hero mysticism. Stimulated by conflict, it is creative.

Finally, there is the highest form of mysticism known as *last-stage mysticism,* or "imminent world-transforming mysticism," which appears in the latter part of the life cycle.

Here, a unity with the world is attained; conflict and the hostile world are eliminated in favor of peace; man becomes a fully integrated being, creatively renewed. He exists in time and in this world—not outside, as in more primitive forms of mysticism. He is in a constant mystical state in which the world and its objects, including his innermost self, are transparent. Now there is no conflict between the Jungian ego and the self, or the conscious and the unconscious. What may appear as hostility to the world is, rather, an intent to recreate and renew it.

*   *   *   *

The attempt in this epilogue to brief the reader on other ways of looking at our subject may threaten to turn confusion into bedlam. The mystic, however, learns to live with paradox, to accommodate himself to opposing views, and finally to unite them. The fullest understanding of mysticism undoubtedly requires a similar effort.

References

1. Phyllis Greenacre. "Penis Awe and Its Relation to Penis Envy" In DRIVES, AFFECTS, BEHAVIOR, R. M. Loewenstein, Ed. (New York: International Universities Press, 1953) pp 176–190.
2. ———. Experiences of Awe in Childhood. *The Psychoanalytic Study of the Child* 11 (1956):9–30.
3. Paul C. Horton. The Mystical Experience: Substance of an Illusion. *Journal of the American Psychoanalytic Association* 22 (1974):364–380.
4. D. W. Winnicott. Transitional Objects and Transitional Phenomena. *International Journal of Psychoanalysis* 34 (1953):89–97.
5. Albert J. Lubin. "From Augustine to Einstein: Some Thoughts on Mysticism, Creativity, and Identity." Paper presented at the San Francisco Psychoanalytic Institute, January 6, 1975.
6. Arthur J. Deikman. Implications of Experimentally Induced Contemplative Meditation. *Journal of Nervous & Mental Disease* 142 (1966):101–115.

7. ———. Bimodal Consciousness. *Archives of General Psychiatry* 25 (1971):481–489.
8. Anton Ehrenzweig. THE HIDDEN ORDER OF ART (London: Weidenfelt & Nicholson, 1967).
9. See reference 5 above.
10. Erich Neumann. "Mystical Man." In THE MYSTIC VISION: PAPERS FROM THE ERANOS YEARBOOKS, Joseph Campbell, Ed. (Princeton: Princeton University Press, 1968) Bolligen Series Vol. XXX, No. 6, pp 375–415.

ACKNOWLEDGMENTS TO CONTRIBUTORS

The program of the Group for the Advancement of Psychiatry, a nonprofit, tax-exempt organization, is made possible largely through the voluntary contributions and efforts of its members. For their financial assistance during the past fiscal year in helping it to fulfill its aims, GAP is grateful to the following:

Sponsors
Abbott Laboratories
J. Aron Charitable Foundation
CIBA-GEIGY Corporation, Pharmaceuticals Division
Maurice Falk Medical Fund
Mrs. Carol Gold
The Grove Foundation
The Holzheimer Fund
Ittleson Family Foundation
Merck, Sharp & Dohme Laboratories
The Olin Foundation
Pfizer Laboratories
The Phillips Foundation
Roche Laboratories
Rockefeller Brothers Fund
Sandoz Pharmaceuticals
Schering Corporation
The Murray L. Silberstein Fund
The Lucille Ellis Simon Foundation
Smith, Kline & French Laboratories
E.R. Squibb & Sons
Bradley A. Stine (in Memoriam)
The Sunnen Foundation
van Ameringen Foundation, Inc.
Leo S. Weil Foundation
Lawrence Weinberg
Weyerhaeuser Foundation, Inc.
Wyeth Laboratories

Donors
Fannie & Arnold Askin Foundation
The Division Fund
Mrs. Walter H. Etzbach
George M. Naimark, Ph.D.
Orrin Stine
The Stone Foundation, Inc.
Edward H. Weiss

OTHER RECENT PUBLICATIONS
GROUP FOR THE ADVANCEMENT OF PSYCHIATRY

No.	Title	Price
96	RECERTIFICATION: A Look at the Issues	$2.50
95	THE EFFECT OF THE METHOD OF PAYMENT ON MENTAL HEALTH CARE PRACTICE	4.00
94	THE PSYCHIATRIST AND PUBLIC WELFARE AGENCIES	2.50
93	PHARMACOTHERAPY AND PSYCHOTHERAPY: Paradoxes, Problems and Progress	6.00
92	THE EDUCATED WOMAN: Prospects and Problems	4.00
91	THE COMMUNITY WORKER: A Response to Human Need	4.00
90	PROBLEMS OF PSYCHIATRIC LEADERSHIP	1.00

Orders amounting to less than $5.00 must be accompanied by remittance. All prices are subject to change without notice.

GAP publications may be ordered on a subscription basis. The current subscription cycle comprising the Volume IX Series covers the period from July 1, 1974 to June 30, 1977. For further information, write the Publications Office (see below).

Bound volumes of GAP publications issued since 1947 are also available which include GAP titles no longer in print and no longer available in any other form. A bound index of these volumes (I through VII) has been published separately.

Please send your order and remittance to: Publications Office, Group for the Advancement of Psychiatry, 419 Park Avenue South, New York, New York 10016.

This publication was produced for the Group for the Advancement of Psychiatry by the Mental Health Materials Center, Inc., New York.